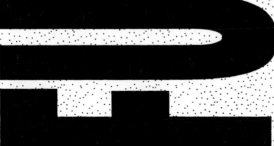

FUGITIVE

HOW TO

RUN,

HIDE,

AND

SURVIVE

KENN ABAYGO

PALADIN PRESS
BOULDER, COLORADO

Also by Kenn Abaygo:

Advanced Fugitive
The International Fugitive

This book is dedicated to all the American servicemen and
women who suddenly found themselves far from friendlies but
who persevered nonetheless and achieved the ultimate goal —
their freedom.

Fugitive:
How to Run, Hide, and Survive
by Kenn Abaygo

Copyright © 1994 by Kenn Abaygo

ISBN 10: 1-58160-754-8
ISBN 13: 978-1-58160-754-X
Printed in the United States of America

Published by Paladin Press, a division of
Paladin Enterprises, Inc.
Gunbarrel Tech Center
7077 Winchester Circle
Boulder, Colorado 80301 USA
+1.303.443.7250

Direct inquiries and/or orders to the above address.

Visit our Web site at www.paladin-press.com

Contents

Acknowledgments

his book was written in part as a result of many years of evasion experience and therefore was influenced by quite a few people, probably none of whom have any idea that they were somehow partially responsible for what you will read in its pages. Many thanks to you all.

The Evasion Mind-Set

Stop. Just stop. Where in the hell do you think you're going, anyway? Heading for the backcountry, eh? Going to drop out of sight for a while, are you? Well, have a swell time, bud. Hope you know what you're doing. Then again, if you don't, it won't matter much. Your plan of disappearing is definitely going to come to fruition, though it might not be quite like you thought it was going to be, with your being *dead* and all. Don't you hate it when a plan doesn't come together?

And *that*, my friend, is the most common problem faced by people who undertake real-world evasion: they fail to plan. Some just don't know any better, being novices in the wilderness and almost totally ignorant of the thorough, intelligent planning required for an effective evasion plan of action. Others *think* they know what it takes, having been trappers, hunters, law enforcement officers, or military personnel. But the fact of the matter is, evasion is an art and science that can take years of practice and practical application to become adept at, not to mention the prerequisite acquisition of knowledge sufficient to get you started. My first experience in evasion came many years ago as a reconnaissance team leader. Today, nearly 20 years later, I find that I am still learning. The evader who has nothing else to learn will not be an evader much longer.

To learn evasion, you have a number of options available to you, some passive, others anything but. This book, the only one of its kind so far as I know, is a passive method of learning evasion. It will give you the knowledge required to evade whoever and whatever you've decided need not bother you anymore. At the other end of the spectrum are various organizations that are more than willing—in exchange for a few years of your life—to give you the practical application part of your evasion education. These are entities with monikers like U.S. Marine Force Recon, U.S. Navy SEALs, U.S. Army Special Forces, and so on. All three will certainly train you well in evasion. However, you may not be willing, for whatever reason, to sign on the proverbial dotted line, especially since all have entrance tests that, well, are a bit extreme, if you get my meaning.

There is another course of action, though. You can take what you glean from this book and practice evasion in your own neck of the woods, desert, plains, swamps, whatever. But before you can put that vital practice to the acid test, you are going to have to learn how to plan.

LOOSE ENDS WILL TRIP YOU UP

The cleverest camouflage and the craftiest evasion shelter will be of limited use to you unless your mind is at ease with what you left behind. Few people can truthfully make the claim that they have nothing and no one to be concerned with. When you begin your evasion, you must first be totally satisfied that every possible loose end has been tied up tight and stands almost no chance of coming unraveled. Interviews conducted by various governments upon repatriation of their prisoners of war clearly indicate that prisoners who had taken steps to provide for the welfare of their families adapted to the rigors of extended incarceration at the hands of a violent enemy much more quickly and easily than those who had left too many things unattended to. Anyone planning an evasion must do the same thing. The evader simply cannot afford to be overly concerned with whom and what he left "back in the world." His mind must be 100 percent on the situation at hand.

If you are legally and/or emotionally attached to anyone, and you intend to remain so during the entire period of your evasion, you must take calculated steps to ensure that person is cared for in your absence. Finances must be dealt with, investments made. Bills are going to have to be paid. It is unlikely that you will be evading forever. This means that unless you intend to change your identity, you are going to have to protect your credit and possessions. This is a tall order that may take years to fill. Remember, you will almost undoubtedly be coming back, be it next month, next year, or a decade from now. You must plan for your return *before you leave.*

Do you have a will? If not, get one. Tomorrow.

Do you need to give someone specific or general power of attorney, so that various legal matters can be handled while you are away? Is that person absolutely trustworthy? General power of attorney means someone has the legal power to speak and act for you in *all legal matters.* This is one hell of a scary thought. Specific power of attorney gives someone the right to act on your behalf on a particular matter, say, to sell your boat if the money starts running out before you get back. You need to think about these things.

You must also arrange to protect your hard-earned credit. Even the wealthiest people on the planet are slaves to credit in one way or another, and you are certainly no different. Bad credit can stay on your record for years. This annoying fact will hamstring you upon your return to society. Every bill you owe has the potential of turning up on the computer files of any number of credit reporting agencies. Being debt-free is a definite advantage when evading. If this is impossible, then you must set up a system for paying your bills in your absence. This can be done by retaining an attorney—and paying him in advance for his services—or enlisting the help of a trusted friend. There is a drawback here: anyone who knows your whereabouts is a potential source and could, inadvertently or otherwise, surrender that knowledge to someone or some organization you are trying to avoid.

WHAT NECK OF THE WOODS?

Regions in which to conduct your evasion are as varied as reasons for evasion itself. You could walk into certain parts of Montana, British Columbia, Maine, Alaska, the Yukon, Idaho, and a plethora of other places and stay gone for years. However, there is no region on Earth that doesn't currently host humans, no matter how remote or inaccessible it appears to be. There are going to be people where you are evading. Count on it.

More important than numbers of people, however, is who and what they are. Twenty hikers cutting through the remote valley you have selected to hide out in are a threat insofar as they may stumble across you, or sign of you, by sheer coincidence. Of greater threat to your continued freedom is the man who comes into the wilderness intending to cut some sign of your presence. This is the professional tracker.

Keep in mind that a professional tracker is not looking for you, but rather searching for signs or clues that indicate your presence in the general vicinity. One partial footprint, a week-old fire site, or a discarded flashlight battery can tell a tracker a great deal. And if that tracker is personally familiar with the area, it just might tell him *enough*.

Remember that a tracker never starts without first analyzing the situation with whatever knowledge he already has about you. He wants you—bad. His reputation rests on his success. His most dangerous weapons are common sense, attention to detail, and an understanding of the human thought process.

Many years ago, two colleagues and I were tasked with finding a small group of men who were evading in southern California. We already had a good idea of their general whereabouts, but the region they were in was fairly large and varied in terrain: rolling hills, mountains, canyons, chaparral, fields, and woods. We narrowed the search down to a single canyon and sat down atop the rim to discuss our options.

It was hot, about 90 degrees. We knew that they would be laying up in as tight a spot as possible until nightfall, when they would start to move again. We had to get them before sunset. I asked Joe where he would be if he were them. He said he'd be in a place no one expected, but that they wouldn't be thinking that way due to their relative inexperience. He said they would probably head for the thicket in the bottom of the canyon, where it is cooler and where they would feel safe. I agreed, as did Don, and we headed down into the canyon.

Not five minutes later, Joe cut some sign in the soft sand of the canyon floor. A moment later, he detected a wire running out of some dense brush, which was part of a booby trap the men had set to deter the likes of us. But it so happened that they couldn't see the area covered by the booby trap from where they were hidden, and that was their final mistake. We were on them like Eskimos on a napping seal.

What all this means is that the perfect evasion area simply does not exist, so stop looking for it. What you want is the area best suited for *your* needs—one with special features that will serve you well in the good times and the bad. This tract must offer reasonable cover during the entire year; seasonal changes in the flora and weather must not have a terribly detrimental effect on your ability to evade without detection. It has to have year-round water sources that you can get at with relative ease. The locale must have terrain that hinders the travel of others yet facilitates your own, and your familiarity with it should allow you to exploit it in such a way as to intimidate any pursuers.

Your selected area must also be able to support you foodwise. Game should be abundant, and you are going to have to familiarize yourself with the indigenous edible, medicinal, and otherwise useful flora. The land should be laid out in a manner that affords you numerous hiding spots, i.e., rugged, broken terrain, preferably heavily wooded, though this is not a requirement. On the other hand, it must also afford you various escape routes that will prove difficult for others to detect, both before and after their use.

Weather is always a concern, but a wise evader will not be deterred by climatic extremes. Survival is an integral part of successful evasion. If you have limited survival skills, your evasion stands a good chance of being unsuccessful and short-lived, indeed. Instead, use bad weather to your advantage just as you would harsh terrain. If your survival skills are up to snuff, you will rejoice at the sight of a severe winter storm while your pursuers head back to civilization.

YOUR MOST DANGEROUS ADVANTAGE

It isn't your weapons. It isn't your training. It isn't the demoralizing terrain in which you have chosen to evade.

What it *is* is your mind—your will to survive and live free no matter how rough it gets. This is the same will that survivors have called on to get them through seemingly unsurvivable ordeals. But just as your pet alligator might turn on you when you're not watching him, your mind can turn on you when all seems lost. Discipline—and a refusal to throw in the towel—will prevent this.

Beware the surfeit of pitfalls that lie in wait for you within your mind. Never assume your evasion will be of a certain length of time. If anything, you must plan for a worst-case scenario and then add a year or two. It is easy to allow your mind to convince you that it is time to return to the light. The facts should convince you, not wishful thinking, unsubstantiated assumptions, and groundless guesstimation.

Be patient.

Chapter 2

Solo vs. the Network

he decision of whether to evade completely unaided by anyone else or to seek or accept assistance may very well be the most important one of your entire evasion.

ALONE IN THE WILDERNESS

Solo evasion is never something to be considered lightly, in any way. Heading into the backcountry, be it for a month or a year, is likely to be one of the most—if not *the* most—grueling, trying undertakings you have ever attempted. Don't kid yourself. It is not going to be fun, amusing, or romantic. Evasion means a temporary—though extended—way of life which is going to find you cold, wet, hungry, miserable, in pain, scared, and hateful. Hateful? You bet. Your mind is going to become fixated from time to time on who and what brought about this tremendous change in your life-style. You will experience a vigorous hatred toward them, be they the IRS, a criminal element (some would say the two are one and the same), or what have you. Don't let that hatred blind you.

One advantage of solo evasion is decision-making; you do it all, and you reap the benefits—or suffer the consequences—of your actions. There is no one else you have to convince regarding a decision other than your own psyche. This saves time, and if the decision you made was a bad one, then you need not be concerned with repercussions from anyone else, though you may have to deal with someone else, namely a pursuer.

Another advantage is security. In solo evasion, you, and only you, know precisely where you are, what you intend to do, where you are thinking about going, and so on. This is a comforting feeling which lends itself to increased confidence as the term of your evasion increases. You aren't concerned with mistakes made by someone assisting you, and you need not worry about someone selling you out for the right price (and everyone has his price).

The disadvantages of solo evasion are just as important as the advantages. You have only yourself to rely upon, for one thing. Some folks prefer it this way; others don't. If you need immediate, no-questions-asked medical assistance, you are going to be out of luck. Your own primitive medical skills will have to suffice. The same is true of food and water, money, communications, and so on. It's only you out there.

THE NETWORK

There are organizations in this country and elsewhere that are designed to assist people like you. Northern Idaho, western Montana, eastern Oregon and Washington state, parts of Wyoming, and other states are home to people who might be willing to give you a hand. This is known as assisted evasion, and it can take many forms.

One of these forms is the Network, which is a secretive, very serious group of people who will feed you, fix you, resupply you, point you in the right direction, and pass you on to the next stop in the Network. I am obviously not going to list their names, addresses, and telephone numbers here; that is going to be up to you to discover and use in as covert a manner as possible. Who are these people, and why might they be willing to help you? It doesn't matter now, does it? Just know that they are there, living their quiet lives on ranches, farms, in cabins, in well-appointed homes in the suburbs, and elsewhere, waiting for you to contact them.

If you are an innocent evading capture by ATF agents or some other agency bent on incarcerating you, and you manage to get into the "Net," you must understand that these people are taking a grievous risk in harboring you. Your innocence may be irrelevant to the government; therefore, the people in the Network are probably going to be arrested right along with you if you are taken into custody. This is something you must consider before you contact your doorman (the first link in the Network).

Conduct while in the "Net" is crucial to the outcome of your stay. Your first priority is security, and this is kept by doing whatever your hosts say, immediately and unquestioningly. Should you hesitate or question the orders of your host, the consequences may be fatal.

Your attitude is extremely important. If they ask you why you are evading, tell them. The chances are excellent that they already know why you are there, and if you try to bullshit them, you run the risk of eviction from the Network. These people are putting themselves on the line for you. If they ask about your history, be honest. However, most will not ask, wanting to stay as distant from you as possible, while still helping. Many folks feel that the less they know about you the better. If they are brusque with you, don't be offended. Though they may seem "put out" by your presence, remember that they are nevertheless willing to help you.

You may not be allowed entrance to their home. Instead, you might find yourself in a bunker below the hog pen, in a hidden alcove above the hayloft, or in the back room of a general store. You stay there until told to go elsewhere. Period. You don't come out to relieve yourself, ask for a drink of water, or complain about the food or lack thereof. You keep your mouth shut and your head down. They have you in a particular spot for a good reason: security. If you make yourself a security threat . . .

This is the active Network we have been talking about. The passive "Net" is much more subtle, posing substantially less risk to the people who help you, but still being very useful. The passive "Net" is loose, consisting of anyone who ignores your presence and denies having seen or heard of you to anyone who asks. For instance, if you were spotted by a ranch hand as you passed through a canyon, and he didn't so much as give you a second look, though you know damn well he saw you, and he doesn't tell a soul about the incident, you have just passed through the passive Network. Many people still believe that ignorance is bliss in cases such as this, and that a man's business is his own, so long as it doesn't threaten or harm them or their family.

The decision to go solo or enter the Network is one that you are going to have to live with. Accept the consequences of your actions, use common sense, practice security, and never do anything that might be considered remotely hazardous to others.

Chapter 3

Physical Conditioning

Doing some jumping jacks, sit-ups, and jogging now and then isn't going to cut it. To be physically ready to conduct an evasion, you are going to have to be thoroughly conditioned. This means you will be able to run five miles—with your pack and weapons—over broken terrain, uphill, without slowing down due to exhaustion. And when you get to a safe spot, you are going to have to be ready to fight or run some more. Maybe even swim a mile or so.

Being in sound physical condition means much more than running ability. It encompasses competent swimming ability, prolonged hiking, short-distance high-speed sprinting, gear hauling, slope climbing, hand-to-hand combat, knife fighting, tree climbing, and literally every other possible physical act you may be required to perform. That is one hell of a list, too.

BIPEDAL LOCOMOTION

Those two legs of yours are among your most valuable assets. They will carry you over fallen logs, through dense brush, across ice floes, over the surface of a lake, and anywhere else you ask them to, provided you have taken care of them. Weak legs will kill you.

Listen, I don't want to turn this book into a fitness manual, but this is important. You have to be in a decent state of physical readiness if you intend to become an evader. Your legs are what are going to be hauling you around. Building strong legs that will carry you fast and far takes some time, but not as long as you might think. There is no need to try and become an Olympian. However, you must be in good enough shape to be able to outrun, outclimb, and outhike anyone who might be after you, including people who have been in the neck of the woods you intend to be in all of their lives.

Start from the feet and work up. Ankle flexes to the sides, up and down, and in circles, increase your foot's ability to negotiate rocky and otherwise jumbled terrain. Wear the heaviest set of boots you own while doing these stretching exercises, but start slowly. Don't jump right in with an hour of these stretches; you won't be walking very far the next day. Stair climbing is another must. You can walk, jog, and eventually run up and down stairs, which will definitely build your ankle and calf strength. A stepping machine is a good item to buy if you have the cash (they aren't that expensive).

When working on the lower legs, you may develop shin splints, which is the muscle pulling away from the bone. It is very painful, but you can stop the pain by tightly wrapping tape around your shins. This means you are going to have to shave your shins, if you don't want to grimace in pain every time you remove the tape (as it removes your leg hair).

The knee has been said to be the worst-designed joint in the body. I can believe it. In my profession (the military), knees go bad with ridiculous regularity, keeping the orthopedic surgeons busy. Pain is your body's warning system. If you fail to pay attention to it, it might bring you to a sudden stop at the worst possible moment. Knee pain means trouble.

An evader with bad knees must stop the pain using any method available. Since I haven't had the chance to have the ortho guy cut on me yet, I take Motrin. This over-the-counter drug stops my knee pain for hours on end, even during long runs with pack, weapon, and other equipment. When knee pain starts to slow me down in the wilderness, I use medicinal herbalism if I have no store-bought drugs.

The upper legs contain some of the body's largest, most powerful muscles. Running, sprinting, speed walking, and a progressive hiking program will build these large muscles and give you stamina for the long haul. Squat exercises are also very effective, but avoid squatting where the upper leg bends below the 180° plane; this can cause serious knee injuries.

The upper torso contains the most vital organ in your body pertaining to physical fitness: your heart. This pump makes your legs go faster and further, your arms lift more weight, your back stronger, and virtually every other part of your body more fit. A strong heart is able to pump blood more efficiently. This blood carries oxygen to the muscles, which, when conditioned, will use the oxygen more efficiently. It is a system, in other words, that will serve you well if you take care of it.

Put the cigarettes away. Forever. I'm not going to preach to you about the evils of smoking. But cigarettes will slow you down by seriously impeding the heart's ability to do its job. Besides, you aren't going to be strolling down to the local 7-11 to buy a carton of smokes during your evasion. Lose 'em.

To build strength in your upper body, I stress calisthenics and weight training, used to complement each other. Today's high-tech weight machines are outstanding, and qualified instructors are usually available to help you get started. If you can't lift your own weight on the bench press, you need to work on your upper body. Calisthenics done at high reps will build your endurance by getting that heart pumping.

Your local book store will have a book or two that will allow you to set up a program for yourself.

THE WET STUFF

An evader who isn't competent in the water is neglecting an aspect of evasion that he simply can't afford to neglect.

Partner, you may have to swim for it. Every evader should be able to swim a mile while dragging his waterproofed gear behind him. He should be able to swim at least 50 meters under water, ending with the same breath he started with. Yes, one breath for 50 meters. Huh? There's no way you can do that? Wrong. Anyone can if he understands technique, is in good cardiovascular shape, and has the need. Get down to the pool and ask an instructor to give you a hand. He or she should instruct you in the simultaneous use of your arms in a modified breast stroke arm action and the leg action that you find is most useful to you. This might be a downward scissors kick, a breast stroke kick, even a dolphin kick. Underwater swimming should be done as deep as possible, utilizing the increased water pressure to your advantage. It's like squeezing a watermelon seed between your fingers; the harder you squeeze, the farther and faster the seed will squirt out from your fingers.

Underwater swimming is just as much a mental exercise as a physical one. Your mind is going to start screaming for the body to surface for air. It does this due to the depleted oxygen level in your blood. CO_2 is what tells your brain that it is time to tell the body to breathe. As it increases, so does the urge to breathe. You can beat this urge through practice and discipline. You can also hyperventilate before ducking under, which overloads your bloodstream with oxygen. What this does is trick your brain into thinking that you don't need to breathe. Unfortunately, hyperventilation dramatically increases your chances of a shallow-water blackout. Avoid hyperventilation, unless you want to become fish food.

MORE TO COME

In this chapter, I have mentioned injuries and medicinal herbalism, both of which will both be covered in detail later on. But before we move on, you should know that physical conditioning prevents many injuries, and that is what you want. It increases your resistance to injury, speeds your recovery, and raises your agility level.

Tod Schimelpfenig and Linda Lindsey, two of the

National Outdoor Leadership School's (NOLS) top instructors, point out in their book NOLS *Wilderness First Aid* (Stackpole Books, 1991) that common causes of backwoods injuries include stream crossing (hopping from rock to rock), putting on a backpack, lifting kayaks and rafts, falling while skiing with a pack, stepping over logs, hiking with a pack, bending over, and shoveling snow. These are all activities an evader could find himself doing. Your being in shape will reduce the chances of injuries like these laying you up or putting you down.

Chapter 4

Principles of Wilderness Evasion

We can break evasion down into a number of principles, no one of which is more important than the other. First is the principle of contemplation, which begins when you first consider evasion as a potential plan of action. This principle can be considered the first step in evasion—mere thought. What goes through your head during this time is likely to have a major effect on your actions in the near future.

Before you make any decisions during this time, you must look at your predicament in as objective a manner as possible. Don't let emotion cloud your judgment. This principle (or phase, if you prefer) will find your mind racing at the proverbial mile a minute. You have to be especially careful not to commit any irrational or otherwise ill-advised acts. Seek the advice of others whose judgment you trust. Listen to them, weigh the facts, and make your decision, but never do so lightly.

The next principle is preparation. This principle is the foundation of all that will follow. What you accomplish during your evasion preparation will dictate by and large what the outcome of your evasion is, be it capture, death, or freedom.

There are four primary issues here: staying alive, remaining undetected, reentry into society, and regaining whatever you left behind.

STAYING ALIVE

You can't expect to evade successfully unless you are adept at hard-core wilderness survival. Your ability to build a fire utilizing primitive means, set useful traps and snares, find and render water potable, employ signals, use primitive first aid, construct a sound shelter, and navigate through the wilderness via the stars, terrain, and other natural assets, is essential to your successful evasion, cut and dried. If you can't do all these things, don't even think about evasion.

Hey, did you think this was going to be easy? Did you assume that this book was going to tell you how to become an evader without your first achieving a certain level of competence? If you did, you may as well put this book down now. You stand no chance of becoming an evader.

Survival and evasion are synonymous. One simply does not exist without the other. No, I am not going to instruct you in the art of wilderness survival within the confines of this book. If you want to learn survival, contact Paladin Press and request a catalog, or ask that your correspondence be forwarded to me and I'll see what I can do.

REMAINING UNDETECTED

The length of your evasion will be determined by limitless factors; however, one thing is for certain: your evasion will be much shorter than you expected unless you adhere to strict rules regarding camouflage, concealment, and security.

Silhouette yourself once, and your evasion is over. Move through an open field once, and it is all over. One reflection from your compass, and that's all she wrote. Let your shadow show up in an aerial photograph, and you'll be captured before you know it. Get my drift?

Let me tell you something—you cannot afford to make mistakes. And if you do get away with a mistake now and then, you will become lazy and begin to make more and more mistakes. You are your own worst enemy. Human nature is not something that works in your favor. Human nature tends to draw you toward a life of ease. Evasion and the easy way are a contradiction in terms. Come to grips with that right now.

REENTRY INTO SOCIETY

Before you leave, you must prepare for your return. Failure to abide by this rule will result in a surfeit of potentially unconquerable obstacles. The old saying about it being unwise to burn bridges behind you applies here. No matter how tempting it may be, don't needlessly destroy any personal or professional relationships or arrangements. The bridge you burn the worst will be the one you need first and most.

It would be improvident to write a letter to the IRS informing it of your disdain for it in a graphic and memorable manner before you commence your evasion.

Organizations and individuals have long memories, and revenge plays a pivotal role in many lives. Exterminating someone is also impolitic, since murder will guarantee you pursuit—pursuit by several law enforcement agencies, which may very well include the FBI. You don't need that, regardless of how badly someone deserves to die. Besides, there are much more enjoyable ways of getting even which don't involve murder, though the malice in these acts and the mayhem they create could be considered illegal.

Maturity and good judgment are what you need to demonstrate when preparing for your evasion. Don't indicate to anyone what you plan unless he is an integral cog in your support system. It doesn't take a space shuttle mission specialist ("rocket scientist" is out) to figure out that you may be about to skip town—and a whole lot more—after you walk into work and tell everyone within earshot to kiss your ass, among other things.

Subtlety is crucial to your successful departure.

RECLAIMING YOUR MATERIAL WORLD

As in reentry into society, reclaiming your material world, i.e., your possessions, is largely a matter of law. Thorough preparation will go a long way toward making this easier.

Most of us, I'd dare say, have a love-hate relationship with lawyers. They provide essential services to us, yet make us pay through the nose for them. However, a good lawyer is often worth the money he or she charges, and this means you should have what you left behind waiting for you when you return, provided the lawyer's retainer was sufficient.

Marriage can be a help, or it can be a hindrance. Your spouse may be waiting at the door for you upon your triumphant return, a big, fat pot roast simmering in the oven (your favorite), or the Malarkey family may be living in what used to be your house, your spouse having divorced you for abandonment and taken much more than your shirts to the cleaners. Ouch.

People change. Lives go on. Believe it.

AREA AND ROUTE RECONNAISSANCE

As you reconnoiter potential evasion sites, you must take special care not to draw unwanted attention to yourself or let on why you are doing what you are doing. Security is critical.

Consider a disguise, preferably a simple one, as these are often best for your area and route recon. Change the length of your hair, grow or lose the mustache or beard, change your eyeglass style if you wear them (or buy a pair of plain glass glasses), dress in a fashion you normally wouldn't (but not in a manner that would make you memorable), and alter your accent (speaking only when absolutely necessary). In other words, be nobody special.

Your vehicle should be a rental, paid for with cash (this reduces the paper trail). Nothing fancy.

In your evasion area, stay off the trails. Move slowly, watching for signs of others. Be focused; check the area well for the factors that will determine its usefulness as an evasion area. Don't dawdle. When your business is done, leave. Take a different route back (out of the woods and on the way home). Never stay in the same place twice. Pay all your bills in cash (fives, tens, and twenties).

ADAPTABILITY AND OPPORTUNITY

These two principles are obviously linked. The most cunning evader out there is the coyote. Here is the master of adaptability, the greatest opportunist on the face of the Earth. He understands these principles and applies them every day of his life. The coyote survives in a vast array of environments—from deserts to the great plains, from cities to rugged mountainous regions—and does so by exploiting what comes his way. He readily adapts to sudden changes and rarely misses an opportuntiy to improve his chances of survival. If you can think and act like a coyote, you will do well.

Evasion has a way of making you adapt and recognize opportunities when they present themselves. (Survival does the same thing.) If you fail to adapt, your evasion comes to an end. If you fail to take advantage of every opportunity, your evasion will be substantially less comfortable and much more annoying and frustrating. (This is not to say that comfort is essential to evasion.) Firsthand experience in the wilderness will provide you with the ability to adapt faster than a novice. *There is no substitute for experience.*

Opportunity knocks more than once. Yes, more than once. However, it may knock but once for a given situation. Of all the time I have spent in the north woods, I have never run across a moose that was about to die of a brain worm infestation. But this was precisely what happened to a friend of mine. He reported it to the local game warden, who split the moose with him. Opportunity. And luck? Absolutely! I have found that those who adapt and take advantage of opportunities often have a way of making their own luck.

Opportunity is something you should tend to before your evasion, too. Get some training in wilderness survival and evasion. You'll thank me later.

REASONS FOR GOING

The reason(s) you left in the first place will continue to play a role in how your evasion terminates. Like the *will to survive*, you must have the *will to evade*. Never forget that your evasion was well planned, and that you had a very good reason for going. As time passes, these factors sometimes become muddled, as a result of loneliness, sagging morale, whatever. Discipline—and a strong sense of purpose—will keep you on the straight and narrow. Try not to lose sight of your objective(s); once you do, your continued evasion is in jeopardy.

Chapter 5

The Hide

I could see his boots, and I noted that he had inadvertently missed an eyelet with his right boot lace, which looked to be constructed of rawhide. Perhaps he had gotten dressed in the dark, or perhaps he was just in a hurry. In any case, I suspected he wasn't out here hunting, but rather looking for me.

A moment after he walked up beside me and stopped—about 2 feet away from where I lay—he rested the butt of his rifle on the cold, moist ground next to his right foot. It had a folding paratrooper stock, which confirmed that he wasn't after game, at least not in the traditional sense. I couldn't see any higher than his shin, and I couldn't see any more of the rifle than the stock, but I suspected it was a Soviet AKM or perhaps a Chinese Type 56.

It was at that precise moment that I realized I had stopped breathing.

My entire body was still, not so much frozen in terror—though I was admittedly somewhat concerned he might discover me—as I was keenly aware of my situation and his alarmingly close proximity. I forced myself to slowly, silently exhale and began to take deep, slow breaths with my face less than an inch from the decaying leaves I was lying on so that my breath wouldn't condense in the chill air and rise like an apparition from the detritus covering my body, which would instantly result in my being discovered.

It seemed at the time that he had stood there for hours, but in reality he was only there a few moments before he moved on, heading up the ridge to the north. The sun was falling rapidly from the sky by now, and after an hour the blackness enveloped me and the creatures of the night began to emerge from their diurnal sanctuaries. A deer of some sort drifted by, stopping every few steps to prick up its ears and sniff the night air. It was absolutely silent as it moved through the forest understory—taking its time, watching, listening, sniffing . . . sensing.

I took the deer's cue and slithered out of my hide after the animal passed. Silently donning my gear and checking my weapon, I pulled the "door" to the hide over the entrance hole—the door being a limb that had fallen from a tree in the storm the day before—and then let the roof's main beam gently down onto the ground, effectively and quietly destroying the shelter. If someone wandered by, the old hide would appear to be just so much more natural debris, which was precisely what it had looked like while I was in it. I dropped the main beam to be sure no one discovered the hollow beneath the foliage and branches.

I couldn't make out the stars through the thick canopy, but it didn't matter; my compass immediately told me which direction to move in, and I did so, moving softly through the forest, watching, listening, sniffing . . . sensing.

That long ago day saw my hide, a.k.a. evasion shelter, kept me free to evade another day. It took me only an hour or so to construct it, and then another 40 minutes to emplace the path guards and "detours" that were supposed to keep people away from the hide itself—devices that obviously failed, given the man standing 2 feet from my head. I never did find out precisely where he approached from, obviously, but as I traveled farther on that night and during the nights that followed, the annoying question kept popping into my head: what approach had I missed or failed to cover effectively with a path guard or detour? My oversight or callousness had very nearly cost me dearly.

The ability to build or prepare an effective hide is only one of a surfeit of skills the evader must possess and be able to demonstrate readily.

Though no single evasion skill is always preeminent, the evader's ability to construct a sound, clever hide is essential to his continued freedom. Cutting corners and assuming safety are two of the evader's most dangerous, potentially fatal mistakes. The hide must be built perfectly every time, and the path guards and detours emplaced along the natural routes of travel to the hide site must be subtle yet trenchant. Planning and strict attention to detail are two of the evader's most precious assets.

THE BLISSS FORMULA

One of the easiest devices I have found for remembering the factors an evader must account for when constructing a hide is the acronym BLISSS:

B—Blend In

L—Low in Silhouette

I—Irregular in Shape

S—Small

S—Survivable

S—Secluded

This acronym is used by the Department of Defense SERE (Survival-Evasion-Resistance-Escape) School System to teach high-risk-of-capture military personnel—Navy SEALs, Army Special Forces and Rangers, Air Force para-rescue specialists and Force Reconnaissance Marines, among others—during the infamous SERE training sessions in California, Washington, Maine, and North Carolina, where the four SERE schools are located. They use it for one reason: it works.

At these schools, students are required to construct and live in hides in regions where SERE instructors know them to be hiding. Though the schools are quite secretive, it is widely believed that the instructors evaluate the hides ("evasion shelters" to them) during the "scenario" and make "corrective criticism" on the spot.

BLEND IN

In other words, your hide must "fit in," camouflage-wise, with its surroundings. This means that the evader must ensure strict adherence to the myriad facets of camouflage principles and techniques. A minuscule texture error, a small mistake in pattern, the most paltry glitch in tone—all can draw some *very unwanted* attention your way and bring your evasion to a swift and final conclusion. Can't have that, now can we?

When selecting materials to build your hide, you must take several factors into account. The material selected must appear natural, not unusual or out of place. It must not draw attention to itself. It should be garnered well away from the hide site itself, because missing vegetation is easy to detect. A branch torn from a shrub leaves the inner, light-colored wood of the shrub exposed and easy to see; a log taken from the forest floor leaves a depression in the ground (logs don't get up and walk off by themselves); a bush uprooted may leave clumps of dirt behind in plain view (dirt clods decorating the forest floor for no apparent reason make people curious). Even if all your materials were found 500 meters from the hide site, you must take steps to conceal your presence in the general area. That light-colored wood glowing in the understory from where you removed a branch from a shrub can be masked with a dab of dirt or mud. (Branches taken from bushes and trees should be small, thus making their absence less conspicuous.) Avoid taking logs from the ground and leaving telltale depressions for all to see and speculate on. Usually, a log from a blow-down that is not in contact with the ground will suffice and be much less noticeable when removed. Live bushes and even saplings can be very useful. Gently pull them free of the ground and cover the hole with natural debris. Several live bushes placed on the roof of your evasion shelter in a natural, unobtrusive manner can fool the best of them.

As your hide begins to take shape, step back from it frequently to see how it looks from several different angles and viewpoints. Study it with your peripheral vision, too; don't just stare at it straight on. If something catches your eye, tend to it. Also, remember to look at the hide from above; don't forget that those looking for you—or more likely, signs of your having passed that way—may have aircraft to assist in their search efforts.

If you utilize man-made items (e.g., cordage, a tarpaulin, a brown garbage bag, etc.), you must take special precautions to ensure that they don't clash with the natural surroundings of the environment you find yourself in. Dirt and mud applied carefully and vegetation used discreetly can help.

LOW IN SILHOUETTE

Forget the teepee, okay? The great masters of evasion, our Native Americans, never hid in their traditional shelters, be they teepees, hogans, lodges, or what have you. They slept, ate, and made little Native Americans in them, but they did not use them to evade their many enemies. Your hide must be low to the ground, not silhouetted against the sky or any other contrasting background. Comfort is your last consideration when constructing a hide, and if you have to crawl into your hide on all fours, or slink down into it like a snake, then so be it.

What you want is a hide that is just high, wide, and long

enough to accommodate you and your gear. You also want to place it in such a way as to be able to see what is going on around you and hear what is happening. In my experience, more often than not it is wise to build upslope, say, three-quarters of the way up a hill or ridge, rather than in the valley itself or in the lowlands. Sounds travel uphill quite well, and it is obviously easier to scope out the surrounding country-side from a high vantage point. In addition, the higher up you are the faster your hide will warm. But the winds you will be subject to may be greater than below, or less. It depends on the local geography. A low-built hide will warm more quickly than a tall one, and it will withstand the rigors of the wind better, too.

IRREGULAR IN SHAPE

Nature has given us many shapes, and the human eye is accustomed to quickly recognizing those which seem out of place in a given environment. How many perfect rectangles, squares, or circles have you come across in the wild? Even a tree's trunk isn't perfectly circular. And when a tree collaps-es in the forest, or a rock crevice is created, it is not symmet-rical. It is haphazard, jumbled. That's the idea where shape is concerned.

Oftentimes, nature provides for you in a big way. The ready-made hide is frequently the best you can get. They blend in perfectly, are low in silhouette, irregular in shape, and so on, and they often can be made very survivable with just a little fixing up.

In the winter of 1993, a young couple and their five month-old baby became stranded in the northern Great Basin desert. Their remarkable story was all over the news, and you proba-bly heard about them (Jim and Jennifer Stolpa). Jim stashed his wife and baby in a tiny cave—barely that, really—at the foot of an escarpment, which measured about 6 feet wide, 5 feet long, and 2 1/2 feet high. The entrance was only 2 feet high and was hardly noticeable from any distance. Two sagebrushes could have been pulled in front of the opening and you would never have known the grotto was there. It complied beautifully with the BLISSS formula.

Wooded lands provide blow-downs that can be used as a hides. I used to teach evasion for a living and have seen all manner of hides, but one of the best was a hollow log amid a large blow-down. The student who found it knew a good spot when he saw one and moved right in. The only modification it needed was a door to cover the entrance, and this was provided by a fir sapling that he transplanted from a spot in a thicket a few hundred meters away.

The bobcat that was in the log when the student moved in, however, didn't think it appropriate for the human to share his quarters. But what could have been a nasty turn of events ended safely, though comically, when the student let out a scream and the cat bolted out the narrow end of the log.

The point here is to make sure any wildlife that is currently using a hide you want to jump claim on is removed *before* you set up shop. In dark, dank spots like hollow logs and blow-downs, I can assure you that some sort of animal—be it insect, reptile, mammal, whatever—is going to be living in there.

SMALL

As previously discussed, the size of your hide should be just enough to hold you and whatever equipment you have along. Never leave any of your gear outside the shelter while you are constructing it or are inside. Keep *your kit with you at all times.* Why? If you suddenly have to flee the area, you don't want to be screwing around running back to your hide to retrieve your things. A pack hanging off a tree outside your hide is a magnet for attention.

You may want to cook while inside your hide. This can be done with your body inside but the fire outside, via a Dakota hole at the mouth of the hide. (This consists of two holes, one about 1 foot deep and 8 to 10 inches wide and the other just as deep but only 4 to 6 inches wide, connected by a 10-inch tunnel running between their bottoms. If you look at this as a cross-section, it looks like the letter U. See Chapter 6 for more detail.) This way, should someone approach as you are cooking, you can snuff out the below-ground fire quickly, and you are already in the hide itself, eliminating the need to scurry back to safety. This system also eliminates the need to enlarge your shelter in order to accommodate a fire.

SURVIVABLE

Your hide must be rugged—tough enough to withstand the rain and snow, wind and sun, heat and cold. Do not build for comfort; build for survival.

One ingredient in building a survivable hide is often simplicity itself. Too elaborate a hide can become its own undoing. Use firm wood, not stuff that has been lying there for years and has gone to rot. (However, small pieces of rotten wood can be used for camouflage, provided they are not used structurally.)

No one part of the hide is more important than another. The walls must be just as solid as the roof beams, and the roof itself must be just as watertight as the walls. The door must be just as resistant to wind as the roof.

Usually, however, when it comes to structural matters, most evaders make their mistakes on the roof. Gravity is your enemy when it comes to rain, and that rain is going to find its way into your hide through the roof unless you construct the tightest roof you possibly can. Thatching is a skill you must become especially good at. A tightly thatched roof is essential to keeping you dry. If it starts to sleet and the temperature is 34°F, that icy rain stands a good chance of making you hypothermic. A well-thatched roof for even the smallest of hides requires a lot of thatching material. Spruce, fir, pine, cedar, hemlock, and cypress boughs all make good thatching material. You can also use deciduous boughs, but remember that the larger the leaves the better. Magnolia, elephant ear, water and Chapman oak, red maple, bigtooth aspen, and any other broad leaf will usually serve you well.

Be sure to break up the tone of the roof with additional materials. A solid mass of leaves is not what you want. Rather, break it up with branches and small limbs arranged helter-skelter among the leaves, giving it a more natural appearance. When you gather your boughs, don't take them all from one small area. Denuding a spot of one particular type of foliage—or all the foliage thereabouts—will tell anyone passing by that something funny is going on. A stripped fir sapling is an eye-catcher.

But the most structurally sound hide in the world will be of little use unless it is in the right spot. Site selection is critical. Build upslope from swamps, marshes, and other wetlands. Waters rise fast under various climatic conditions—conditions that you may not be aware of. In the warmer months, insects thrive around water. You don't need mosquitoes carrying you off in the middle of the night. Look upslope before you build. Is there any evidence of avalanche or landslide proclivity? Could the next rain bring that precariously perched boulder down on top of you?

SECLUDED

Humans are creatures of comfort and habit. Most will only do what has to be done and no more. If they don't have to go into that pocosin (an ungodly thicket of swamp found in the Southeast), if they don't have to climb that steep ridge, they often won't. Force Reconnaissance Marines are taught to lay up in "harbor sites," a marine term for a place to sleep. They are taught that harbor sites must be well off the beaten path, if possible in the nastiest, thickest, most intimidating area they can find. The logic is sound; no one wants to venture into bad places unless they absolutely have to. This is the kind of place you want your hide to be in.

Avoid paths, trails, and trail networks like the plague, even if it is clear that they were created by animals. Humans will use those same trails. Avoid building too closely to bodies of water, be they creeks or oceans. Man is drawn to water just as insects are. Stay clear of villages, towns, and any other place that humans are present, even if you see no sign of their presence in the woods surrounding the populace. In short, avoid anything man-made. If he put it there, he'll be back to check on it. Count on it.

Even though it would appear you have chosen the most secluded of sites, silence is crucial. Sound has a way of traveling fast and far. One whack on a tree with your survival knife may echo a long, long way and fall upon ears belonging to someone you don't want around. Go about your business always assuming that someone is close by. Stealth is one of the keys to evasion and survival.

If possible, never sleep in the same shelter or area twice. Saddam Hussein doesn't, and with good reason. Neither should you, for that same reason.

Destroy your hide immediately after use. Leave no evidence of its ever having existed.

When you build your hide, have escape routes in mind that will allow you to slip away without being detected. That route should keep you masked with shadows and any other feature that makes your being seen less likely. Think like a wild animal would. You are one now.

Chapter 6

Food and Water Procurement

While contemplating evasion, it is easy to forget that you are going to be *living* in the wilderness. This means that everything you would be doing back in civilization you will now be doing in the boonies, the difference being that you no longer have all the conveniences civilization offers, and when you do these things, you are going to have to do them without anyone else knowing.

You just read about hide construction, so now it's time to learn about feeding and watering yourself with no one being the wiser.

TRAPS AND SNARES

Though man came from the water many millennia ago, supposedly when he was a salamander, slug, or some such thing, he has largely lost touch with the watery world. Sure, we fish, swim, surf, scuba dive, snorkel, sail, and pursue countless other pastimes on, in, or near the water. But we nevertheless make these forays temporary. The evader can use this to his advantage when it comes to traps and snares.

Since man is terrestrial rather than aquatic, the evader should focus his efforts on trapping and snaring along and in the water. It is actually easy to use effective sets under the surface, therefore keeping any evidence of your presence out of sight of passersby or someone who may be looking for you. Additionally, water is home to myriad creatures that are quite willing to give their lives for you. You don't want to let them down.

INTELLIGENCE IS RELATIVE

As is true with humans, some fish are smarter than others. The best angler in the world can't catch as many black marlin in an hour as I can sunfish. But intelligence is only half of the equation. The other half is population density.

Evasion fishing, like a bass tournament, is a matter of finding the most fish and then figuring out what they want to eat. In bass tournaments, size is important. And though it would be nice to catch a 10-pound bass while evading, the wiser evader goes for sheer numbers. But here we have the added catch of angling in such a way that not a soul knows what you are up to—or that you are even thereabouts.

What the evasion angler is looking for are fish that willingly bite, don't make too much of a ruckus when hooked, are in good number, and are not averse to eating a variety of foods. Some examples of such fish are catfish, carp, panfish (bluegills, sunfish, etc.), suckers, and so on. Note that landlocked salmon, brown trout, muskellunge, pike, largemouth and smallmouth bass, bonefish, haddock, sailfish, and other "glory" fish are not on the wanted list.

If you studied your evasion area thoroughly before you started your little adventure, you will know what fish live there, what they eat, precisely where they live in their aquatic ecosystem, how their habits are affected by weather, season, and even lunar phase, and everything else about them, including when they spawn. You can't afford to *guess*; you have to know. Guessing is for fools.

EASY PICKIN'S

Below is a list of some of North America's most common, easy-to-catch fish and what they like to eat.

• *Catfish (channel, blue, flathead, bullheads, et al)*: nightcrawlers, live or dead baitfish (minnows, etc.), chicken livers (or any other liver), and any aromatic bait. Note that some catfish have very definite preferences.

• *Carp*: corn, worms.

• *Sunfish*: worms, insects, spiders, small minnows.

• *Suckers*: worms, fish eggs.

• *Bluegills*: worms, insects, spiders, small minnows occasionally.

These fish are a mere sampling of what may be available and easy to come by. This is not to say that other, more glamorous fish, like the salmonids and basses (largemouth, smallmouth, rock, redeye, yellow, and white) won't come your way. In fact, if you are evading in Alaska, salmon and trout might very well be your mainstay.

RIGS AND SETS

All evasion fishing rigs and sets have variations. You might have to modify your set to adapt to your situation. As far as design is concerned, there are no hard and fast rules, so long as the set remains covert.

Two-Bush or Stake-Out
This is one of the evader's simplest, most effective sets. In shallow water, run a line between two bushes, heavy reeds, submerged tree branches, etc., below the surface. Off of this line

run several perpendicular lines attached by a prusik knot to prevent slippage. (A prusik knot attaches a vertical rope to a horizontal rope. When under tension, the knot holds fast; when loosened, it slides along the horizontal rope.) Attach a variety of baits to the hooks on each of these lines (there is no rule that says you can have only one hook per line), and set them at different depths by using different length lines and weights if necessary.

The anchor line should be heavy, 20- to 30-pound test. The bait lines can be lighter, but no lighter than 15-pound test. Once the rig is set, stay nearby for half an hour or so, then check it. If you have a fish, take note of which line—and therefore which bait he hit on and what depth it was at (you did remember to keep track of what bait went where, didn't you?)—and then set the rest of the lines at that depth with that bait.

Set other rigs nearby, too. You can have as many in the water as you want.

Sapling Rod

Cut or otherwise acquire a sapling between 6 and 10 feet long. Tie a length of line to the thin but strong tip, bait the hook, and set the "rod" so that it appears to be just another piece of wood along the bank, i.e. the tip should be underwater, giving no hint of what lies below.

This is an easy rig to set and check.

Bank Line

Just affix a long length of line with a hook at the terminal end, bait it, and throw the bait out into a likely looking spot. Tie the other end off to a submerged root or rock, then subtly mark the spot so that you can find it again.

Fish Traps

These are widely varied. However, most use the concave door principle to allow fish to enter the trap but not get out. An easy minnow trap can be made by cutting a liter-sized plastic soda bottle in half width-wise, then inverting the top end into the bottom, so that the neck is down inside the lower half. Bait it with bread, insects (or insect larvae), or whatever else you think will do the trick, and set it in the shallows, hidden. Minnows will swim right in, but most won't be able to get out.

Simplicity is one of the keys to a good fish trap. Placement is the other. The craftiest trap possible will be of little use if it is poorly placed. Again we see the importance of understanding the ecosystem and its inhabitants.

The fish pen is an excellent trap which uses the victim's instincts against it, namely its desire to face upstream in a manner that allows it to conserve energy. In moving water, most fish wait for the food to come to them, which is why they face upstream; they are looking for food coming their way. This might be insects in their larval form (nymphs), such as mayflies, caddis flies, and stone flies, or it could be a smaller fish heading downstream. It might be a terrestrial insect that has fallen into the stream. Whatever the case, the fish pen gives the fish a place to "hold" or wait for that meal. The entire pen must be underwater and in a place that can't been readily seen from the shore. It needs no bait, and must be marked covertly on shore so that you can find it on your rounds.

A wall pen is used in tidal areas, which might be along the shoreline or along a tidal river. At low tide, just before the tide comes in, arrange a rock wall faced toward the beach or bank. When the tide comes in, the fish will move into the pen. Be there when the tide goes out again and remove any fish that may have remained behind. What you have made is a tide pool. Before you run off with your fish, destroy the pen, thus eliminating a big clue as to your whereabouts and activities.

Other Means
Poison is neither a trap nor a snare, but it can be deadly effective. If you are along the beach, gather and burn a bunch

of seashells. Spread the resulting powder (high in lime) in a quiet backwater, eddy, or deep tide pool. It will kill the fish therein. Scarf 'em up and skedaddle.

You can electrocute fish easily with a hand-cranked mini-generator. Just run a copper wire from it into the water and start cranking. Within seconds, you will have stunned fish floating on the surface.

Whatever method you use is fine, so long as it is covert. Security. Security. Security. Security, by the way, is one of the Nine Principles of War, which are directly linked to Sun Tzu's philosophy of war, penned c. 500 B.C. One crafty bugger, indeed.

FOR THE LAND-LUBBER

Good fishing locales may be scarce in your evasion neighborhood. So, you are going to have to dine on elk, moose, deer, wild boar, grizzly, or whatever else presents itself to you for consumption, right?

To use the vernacular, NOT! There is no subtle way to trap, cut, and prepare animals of this size. You are bound to inadvertently leave fur, bone, blood, viscera, or other sign of the animal having been killed there. A good tracker will read these clues like a book and be on you like a senator on an honorarium. Go for the small, dumber, less volatile critters like rabbits and hares, squirrels, voles, muskrats, small beavers (the last thing you need is to get into a brawl with an adult beaver), woodchucks (groundhogs), and other such game.

The problem, however, is setting and checking your traps and snares in a clandestine manner. Again we turn to simplicity and subtlety.

Sets like the twitch-up, Ojibwa bird snare, treadle spring, peg-rock, t-bar, figure-4 deadfall, lever and fulcrum, and ramp snare are overt snares. Using these will get you caught. What you need is a snare that you can watch and still have a good chance of catching game in, but that you can quickly hide or dismantle should someone approach. Any snare that fits this bill will do. If you can hide or dismantle it in one move, it is okay.

DINNERTIME

You are not going to be eating everything you catch raw. By cooking your food, you often make it more palatable and kill germs and bacteria, both of which raise your morale. (Never underestimate this critical aspect of evasion.) But you can't cook your hard-earned chow over a roaring fire unless you want to invite those who are looking for you to join in the festivities. You must cook underground.

This is not to say that *you* are going to be underground. The fire is.

Dakota Hole

Beneath a leafy tree, preferably a thick conifer, dig a hole about 1 foot deep and 8 to 10 inches wide. Dig another 10 inches or so away, just as deep, but only 4 to 6 inches wide. Now connect the two via a tunnel running between their bottoms. If you look at this as a cross-section, it looks like the letter U.

Now, at the bottom of the wider hole, angle your tinder and ignite it. Follow this by small amounts of thin kindling and then fuel. All three levels of fuel—tinder, kindling, and fuel—should be small enough so that the flames never rise above the ground. The smaller hole is your ventilation hole. Without it, the fire won't stay lit. You must apply the fire triangle: oxygen, heat, and fuel. Take one away, and the fire goes with it.

When you are done with the hole, fill it back in with the spoil.

Ground Oven

Dig a hole 1 foot deep or so and about 1 foot wide. Cover the bottom with 3 to 4 inches of hot coals. On top of these, put your food, either in a container filled with water or in aluminum foil. Now put in 2 more inches of coals and cover them with spoil (dirt). Depending on the intensity of the coals and what you are cooking, your meal could be done in as little as half an hour.

THE UNINVITED DINNER GUEST

This is you.

From time to time, you may find yourself in a situation that requires you to borrow food from another person who has plenty. This guy is Farmer Brown.

Farmer Brown has a garden. His garden has tomatoes, potatoes, squash, corn, and lots of other vegetables. You are going to help yourself.

First, take only what you need. Second, take it at night. Third, watch the farm for two days to get an idea of his routine and that of his animals. Be especially watchful for his dog(s). Fourth, never take the best and biggest specimens. Take small ones that he is less likely to miss. And take them from different plants, too. Fifth, take from a position of cover, on your belly, from the outermost rows. Don't go wandering around in his garden. Sixth, don't hit the same farm twice; he will be waiting for you the next time if you left some evidence of your visit. And for God's sake, don't let your conscience talk you into leaving something in return, like a little money. If you are going to do this, skip the stealing and go right to the authorities, turning yourself in. They'll feed you.

HAVE A DRINK

Man is attracted to water like a German to Octoberfest.

With this in mind, you must be exceedingly stealthy when getting water. Even the smallest springs, narrowest creeks, and most obscure marshes draw man. He may not be after the water, however. Maybe he's after the beaver, mink, and muskrat that haunt the pond, swamp, river, or creek. He may be hunting the moose that wade thereabouts or be in search of the waterfowl that stop there during their seasonal migrations. Whatever the case, he's likely to be there at some time or another, no matter how remote the area. If you got there, he can get there, too.

All water should be garnered at night. Not at dawn or dusk, at night. Animals frequent water holes during the hours of dawn and dusk. You spook a 1,500-pound moose, and every resident of the forest for several hundred meters will know it. You flush 500 Canada geese from a pond, and the racket they make will wake the dead.

Get your water as you would garden veggies—quietly, from a position of cover, using the principles of camouflage, in the dead of night, after surveying the area for some time. Purify all water before drinking.

Are we having fun yet?

Chapter 7

The Gang's All Here

Unless you were a hermit monk artist in your other life, you have had to live and work with others. Perhaps you have had to work closely with others for extended periods, say, in the military, as part of a study group, or on a jury. Group dynamics, particularly group *leadership* dynamics, are a tricky, complex subject.

Attempting evasion as a member of an organized group will require you to understand group dynamics. And if you are the leader of this group, then you are really going to have your work cut out for you. Don't kid yourself; this is not going to be easy.

But before we get into evasion leadership, let's take a gander at the pros and cons.

PROS

Group evasion will afford you more eyes and ears with which to evade. This is a major plus! Physical security is not something to be taken lightly.

Several minds are better than one. A bevy of ideas and opinions, viewpoints, and concerns always outweighs the one.

Thorough route and area reconnaissance is made easier when undertaken by a group.

CONS

The larger the group, the greater the risk of detection via sound, sight, and sign.

Group interaction can be adversely affected by any number of variables. More mouths to feed and water. More injuries to care for. More shelters to build. This could lead to compromise (which, in evasion, means discovery).

In other words, the "impact" or "footprint" of a group is much more difficult to conceal.

If a member leaves the group to return to society, the group faces an additional security risk; the returnee may let on—intentionally or otherwise—where the group is, who is in the group, and so on.

FUNDAMENTALS OF EVASION GROUP LEADERSHIP

The leader of a group of evaders is going to be tested on a daily basis. He can't expect his people to behave like a military unit. They aren't a military unit; they are civilians. (If you are a military small unit leader who may find himself in an evasion situation, then the aforementioned does not apply to you.) However, the same fundamentals apply, and you can put them to good use.

You can't ask, direct, or expect your people to do anything that you wouldn't be willing to do yourself. For instance, you can't tell Bill to remove several apples from an orchard unless you have already demonstrated (telling your group you'd do it isn't good enough) your willingness to take acceptable risks for the welfare of the group. This is called leadership by example. What it does is convince your group that you are one of them, willing to do whatever is necessary for the betterment of the group. It shows that you are the type who leads from the front, not from a position of safety in the rear.

The leader must show genuine concern for the welfare of the group, as well as the accomplishment of the mission. The mission is to remain free and undetected. The welfare of the group, since all your group members are human and have real concerns and expectations, is also important. Unless you and your group are marines or other military personnel, the welfare of the group may very well be considered more important than the mission itself. You're going to have to deal with this.

You must know each group member well. A relative stranger in an evasion group is a threat to the group. The leader must be personally familiar with everyone's background, reason for joining the group, skills, quirks, weaknesses, and strong points. Failure to know any one of these could prove disastrous at the worst possible moment. No one can be admitted to the group unless another already in the group can personally vouch for him (or her). We're talking about internal security here.

Traits of the Evasion Group Leader

Effectively leading an evasion group requires numerous leadership traits that will serve the leader and the group well at all times, regardless of circumstances. No leader is going to be able to demonstrate all of these traits all of the time.

From time to time, *every* leader falls short of the mark. The key is to apply as many of these traits as often as possible, and when you fall short, recover quickly.

Consistency is a trait that you can't do without, for an inconsistent leader—one who is erratic and flighty—will be unpredictable to his group. This may seem like a worthy trait (capriciousness) for an evader—and it is, if you are alone—but it dangerous for a group leader. Your group has to know what to expect from you at all times. They have to know how you think and what you would do in a given situation.

Dependability is indispensable to the leader. If you can't be counted on when the going gets nasty, you won't be the leader for long. Dependability applies to physical as well as mental aspects. The evasion group leader has to be able to perform physically under the toughest conditions, and at the same time he has to be able to make logical, correct decisions under extreme stress. Precarious situations are commonplace in evasion.

Attention to detail is a trait many people lack. The fine print, when it comes to evasion, could mean the difference between life and death. The little things have a bad way of turning into big things on a moment's notice. When that big thing manifests itself as a hiker who saw you, and that hiker turns out to be a Mafioso on vacation (and that particular organization is really keen on finding you, for whatever reason), then you have a problem of catastrophic proportions. Followers look for their leaders to show attention to detail. If you take note of the small stuff, then they know the big stuff is going to be tended to as well.

Decisiveness is the lifeblood of the leader. You, as the head honcho, are expected to make decisions every day. You can't waffle or hesitate. You must act, and act quickly. And when you make that decision, you had better stick by it, unless it becomes absolutely necessary to change your mind. This last factor will seldom come into play if you show superior judgment.

How does one acquire good judgment? Experience and knowledge. Judgment is born of both, not just one. The most artful attorney in the yellow pages will fall prey to a novice opponent if he lacks good judgment for the briefest of moments. One lapse, and that's all she wrote. Obviously, common sense goes a long way toward helping the leader develop good judgment.

Tact is a trait that doesn't sit well with many leaders; they think a leader has to be a tyrant, always brusque and overly forceful with his men and women. This is the leader whose followers do so out of fear of repercussions rather than trust and respect. This is the leader you need to get rid of, and fast. The relationship between leader and follower must be one of mutual respect. Tact demonstrates that respect and serves to reinforce the bond between the two.

The leader must always be thorough, too. If you let too many things slip through the cracks, your group will start to question your competency to lead. If you break camp, and five miles into a movement you realize that you forgot to destroy your hide, thus forcing the group to hole up while you and a security team go back to take care of the *security breach* that you caused, you may be out of a job—and an evasion group—when you return.

You will be the judge occasionally, and you had better show an excellent sense of justice. Justice and judgment go hand in hand. Decisions must be just when it comes to discipline within the group, and you must be willing and able to enforce rulings handed down.

The forward-thinking and initiative-oriented leader is a gem. This is the guy who is proactive, not reactive. He sees problems before they actually occur and moves to prevent them. He considers future requirements long before the others and initiates a plan to deal with them. He is a planner.

An evasion group leader is always ethical and bases all his decisions pertaining to judgment and justice on ethics. In other words, he always does the right thing. He never puts his own welfare before that of the group. If you feel this might hinder your survival, I suggest you evade solo. Some folks are better cut out for solo evasion. I'm not passing judgment, merely stating a fact.

A leader carries himself as such and is not hesitant to step forward and accept responsibility. Bearing is vital to the image of the leader.

Your attitude must reflect a willingness for personal sacrifice. Going out of your way to make damn sure the group is taken care of is your job.

Finally, there is loyalty. Group evasion requires loyalty among all its members. Disloyalty besets security problems, which usually beget a calamity.

Well, now you know what to expect as a member of an evasion group. Evasion groups can be a good thing, and they can be anything but. If you use the leadership traits discussed here, you will be okay.

Chapter 8

The Danger Zone

Should you elect to undertake your evasion in an exceedingly remote region, you may not have recurring problems with danger or high-risk zones, such as roads and highways, international borders, and regions with a high human populace. However, you may have to deal with river and stream crossings, glacier crossings, and other treacherous areas that simply can't be bypassed. But let's look at human-engineered danger zones first.

ON THE BORDER

Now, I'm not talking about the U.S./Canadian border. I'm talking about *real* borders, and everything that comes with the territory: heavily armed guards with dogs, automatic weapons, night vision devices, and perhaps even thermal imaging devices. Night vision devices fall into two categories: active and passive. Active devices rely upon their own brightening systems to illuminate the night. Passive devices simply amplify celestial and lunar light. Both are effective and allow the user to see a man in the dead of night. Thermal imaging devices (TIDs), such as the thermal sight used on the TOW anti-tank missile now in use by the U.S. armed forces, do not use heavenly light, but rather heat put out by bodies and equipment. Unlike night vision devices, thermal imaging equipment can see right through smoke, dust, mist, or anything else short of a solid object.

I had the chance to look through a thermal imaging device during the Gulf War, and I can personally guarantee you that it is one hell of a piece of gear. We were picking out kangaroo rats, birds, Iraqis, and their equipment, even under terrible conditions (the dense clouds of oil smoke from the burning oil fields). An evader is going to have a nearly impossible time getting by something like this. My advice is to cross the border elsewhere, where thermal imaging equipment is not in use.

Just how are you supposed to determine whether border guards have TIDs? Observation. Before you cross a guarded border, observe the area you are considering for at least three days. Use your binoculars to scrutinize the gear the guards use. Most TIDs are mounted on a tripod or weapon system and are easily recognized by their unusual appearance and wide optics. The time you spend observing the area also serves to make you familiar with guard patterns of movement, routines, habits, shift changes, and so on. All of this can be put to good use in determining whether this is a good area in which to attempt a crossing.

Night vision goggles (NVGs) might be a little harder to detect, as they aren't brought out until nightfall and are worn on the face. AN-PVS 5 NVGs (the ones used by U.S. forces) are readily available to anyone and just about any country who wants them. They are excellent, but they can't see through fog, smoke, thick dust, and other such things like the TIDs can.

A set of NVGs and a good supply of batteries make an outstanding selection for your evasion kit.

Some evaders claim that their camouflage and concealment skills are so phenomenal that they would simply cross during the day. No matter how good you are, don't try this. Somewhere else on the border there will be a better place that will suffice for crossing at night. Don't let arrogance get you caught.

Being seen is one thing, but being blown up is quite another. Many borders are mined. It goes without saying that mine fields are something to be avoided. However, you may one day find yourself in one. I did, and though I'm in the military, I never actually *expected* to find myself there. I was lucky, though. The area or "lane" in which I crossed the mine field had already been cleared by combat engineers, so I was relatively safe (unless they missed one). Nevertheless, if I never have to do that again, it will be too soon.

Mines can be detonated by pressure, pressure-release, sound waves, ground vibrations, timers, and "on command," which means that someone is monitoring the mine and can detonate it whenever he wishes by electronic means. Which you are most likely to encounter depends entirely on what border you are crossing.

Mines can be equipped to explode and send metal fragments tearing through you with the hopes of killing you or blowing off a foot, to demoralize you and whomever you are with. They can also be rigged with gas, e.g., chemical warfare mines. Ol' Saddam was supposed to have myriad chemical mines waiting for us when we attacked into Kuwait, but few were found. This doesn't mean you won't run into them. Nerve and blister agents are common gas mine fillers. If you even *think* that a certain area might be mined, cross elsewhere. If you can't cross elsewhere, then read the next paragraphs very carefully.

The precise border itself is not your first danger zone. This is the area immediately before the first border in what you might falsely consider to be safe territory. Mines sown in such areas have killed countless evaders. Don't forget this.

False borders are commonly used by numerous nations (naming them would be a security violation) to deceive evaders and insurgents alike. These appear to be the real McCoy but are designed with intentional gaps that make you think you have passed through the danger zone safely—then,

Whump! You're history. Border danger zones must always be considered wider than they appear to the eye.

FENCING SYSTEMS

Fences have been used to keep others out, or in, for thousands of years. The materials used in their construction have changed a bit in the last hundred years or so, and the use of electricity has of course been implemented, but for the most part the philosophy behind their use has remained largely unchanged.

Electricity is something to be reckoned with. Fortunately, you can determine whether a fence is charged in a number of ways. Simple observation is the easiest—and ofttimes the best.

Electrified metal fences require insulators. These will usually be attached to the posts but might also be in between them. Scout the fence line for them.

If the guards are patrolling the fence line with dogs, watch the dogs. If they refuse to come too close to the wire, it may be electrified. Rodents and other animals are sometimes electrocuted. Keep an eye out for their carcasses. If a storm moves through the area, look for electrical arcs along the fence. To see if a fence is charged, touch it with a damp piece of wood, a moist vine, or some other weak conductor. A shock will result if it is charged, but it won't be bad.

Barbed wire is a favorite method of border protection. Even the best barbed wire fence can be breached by an evader, though I will once again *highly recommend* that you select a spot on the border that is not covered by wire, guards, dogs, and other impediments.

You can breach single-strand barbed wire by maneuvering beneath the lowest strand if it isn't run taut too close to the ground. Use a sturdy stick about 2 feet long to push the bottom strand up as you slide beneath it in the supine position. You can use that same stick if the bottom wire is too close to the ground. Carve a notch in each end of the stick and use it as a vertical wedge to pry two wires apart, then slip through them. Take care to wipe out any telltale marks left by your passing. And before you go crawling beneath that wire, probe for mines directly beneath it. This is an old trick that can ruin your whole day in a flash.

More annoying than the single-strand fence is the single- double-, and triple-apron fence. This system uses barbed wire set at angles and at various heights and depths. It takes more time to get through a well-set apron fence. Watch for mines and booby traps rigged within the apron. These might be pressure-activated or designed to go off with a proximity fuze. Negotiate the apron fence in the same manner as you would a single-strand.

You have probably seen photos of razor (concertina) wire in magazines and on television. This is the nasty looking stuff that prisons use to line the tops of walls. It's like a Slinky toy, only much larger and inundated with small, razorlike projec- tions that, like Lizzy Borden, can and will cut you up.

But concertina can also be set right on the ground. It may be staked down with metal engineer stakes, or if the user is lazy, he'll just lay it on the ground. A smart user always uses a minimum of three layers, two running parallel to one another and touching, and the third on top of and straddling the lower two. He won't pull it tight, because this lowers it, making it less effective. And he'll stake it down with metal stakes that are at least 3 feet in length, preferably 5 feet.

You may be required to negotiate a concertina fence— among other things—using a stick and some strips of cloth. Pull the opposing loops of the wire together and then tie them off with the cloth. The 7-foot-long stick is used to lift wire that is not staked down. Once through a set of loops, the evader then removes the cloth, erases his tracks, and moves on to the next loop. It is vital that you remember to remove the cloth strips and erase your tracks. Also, you must probe for mines as you go.

I won't tell you how to negotiate chain link. Chain link is used to protect something important and often has concertina or barbed wire on top. Stay out of chain-link areas.

Other fences may consist of solid walls of wood, logs, or concrete. Such obstacles could have broken glass imbedded in the top of the wall, so don't just jump up there. Feel the top first. When you go over it, don't vault. Keep your profile low.

PROBING FOR MINES

Mines along borders are usually detonated by pressure or pressure-release, though more advanced countries might use fancier stuff. Antipersonnel mines (the ones designed to blow off your foot, leg, hand, or arm) don't require much to set them off. You better find them before they find you.

Rule #1: If you find one mine, you'll find another.

Rule #2: Trip wires are not always set at ankle height.

Rule #3: Don't try and remove a mine; it may be rigged with a mercury switch that detonates the mine when it is moved. Go around it.

Rule #4: The place you least expect to find a mine is precisely where a mine will be.

Rule #5: A well-laid mine field will channel you into a more dangerous area. Move against the grain.

When crawling through an area sown with below-ground mines detonated by pressure and/or above-ground mines set off by pressure-release (trip wires), you are going to need two simple tools: a fixed-blade knife and an 18-inch-long stick.

The knife is used to probe for below-ground mines. Hold the knife in the palm of your open hand, palm up. At an angle of about 30°, probe the ground with the blade, sliding it into the ground slowly and evenly. Probe in an arc in front of you, making a swath 1 foot wider than you are on each side. It is important to hold the knife in such a way that if you strike a mine, the knife will slide up your palm, not move the mine in any way.

Trip wires are found (hopefully) with the stick. As you crawl along, hold the stick out in front of you between your thumb and forefinger, at one end of the stick, so that it can swing slightly. If it touches a wire, it will bounce off it gently.

WARNING: A dirty trick is to place several below ground, pressure-detonated mines right after the trip wire and onto the mine. Probe before you go over the wire.

Below-ground mines can sometimes be spotted by eye. Look for spoil and dirt discoloration. After a storm, shallow mines may become exposed. Guards patrolling mine fields will often wear paths down through the field; they know where the mines are and aren't.

NATURAL OBSTACLES

What nature throws in your path may be more formidable than what man does. Icy rivers and streams, snake- and alligator-infested swamps, seemingly impenetrable pocosins, towering mountain ranges, or other obstacles will be waiting for you. It is not nature that kills evaders, but rather the evader's inability to deal with nature on her terms. I have crossed huge mountain ranges in Korea, broiling deserts in Arabia, screeching jungles in the Philippines, and an array of other natural obstacles, and I am no different than you. Let me say that again: *I am no different than you.*

In my former job as a recon team leader, I frequently found myself crossing streams, creeks, rivers, bays, and other bodies of water. I can personally attest to the fact that water will kill you quick if you misjudge it. Water crossings gone bad cost untold lives every year. Even more are killed when caught in the water unexpectedly, such as in a boat sinking, flash flood, or fall. Most people make the mistake of trying to fight the water or thinking that it isn't as dangerous or powerful as it really is. Such underestimation will end your evasion permanently.

One of the most treacherous natural obstacles you will cross as an evader is a river, particularly a river with noticeable current or rapids. To get to the other side safely and quietly, you must plan, and plan well. You must take effective safety precautions and have a back-up plan for when the primary goes downstream like you are about to.

If you must wade across, select the ford with the most slack water. Rapids—and their little brother, riffles—no matter how small they seem, will sweep you off your feet in a heartbeat. Once you are heading downstream, stopping becomes exponentially more difficult. Use a wading staff to probe the bottom ahead of you, checking for slick rocks, holes, soft bottom, submerged logs, and other nuisances. Keep your weight distributed slightly upstream. As you near the far bank, don't rush. Continue on evenly.

In less rambunctious water you should use a flotation device of the natural kind. A dry log decorated with a few dabs of brush, with you hanging onto the side, can mask your profile well. Most evaders using this tack make the classic mistake of swimming the log directly from one side of the river to the other. Have you ever seen a log leave one bank and head straight across the river to the far bank? No? Neither have I. Such a sight would certainly draw attention.

Instead, leave the bank gently, skirting the near shore, slowly and inconspicuously moving out toward the center. The only part of your body used for propulsion is your legs, well below the surface. A modified breast stroke kick is usually good. Take your time and drift with the current, trying to appear as natural as possible. When you reach the far bank, slip beneath the log and let it go. You stay there and quietly crawl ashore.

Have you considered the water temperature? If it's cold you are going to have to waterproof your gear well so that you can get an immediate change of clothes once ashore. It would be embarrassing to die of hypothermia at this point.

While you are slithering up the bank is not the time to wonder what is on this side. You should have checked your map (map reconnaissance) and observed the far bank *before* you set out for it.

Did you remember to wipe out your tracks on the other bank?

You didn't pull that log out of the ground and leave a deep impression, did you? Logs don't get up and walk off by themselves.

Mountainous terrain is normally what an evader pictures when he thinks of good evasion territory, and he is often right. However, ranges often present the evader with obstacles that can make a grown man cringe. But you need not be a master mountaineer to safely negotiate them.

Your first consideration is weather. Mountain ranges make their own weather systems. What is happening in a low valley at one end of the range is *frequently* radically different from what's going on at altitude, on passes, on the other side of the range, and so on. Assumptions will kill you when it comes to mountain weather.

Mere meters in elevation, and seemingly inconsequential terrain features, have a way of altering highly localized weather patterns in a matter of minutes, if not seconds. This was clearly demonstrated to me in the winter of 1992 while I was operating in the Maritime Alps of southeastern France. My group left the base camp just after sunrise one January morning, heading down the valley for a large meadow. A 50-foot drop in elevation raised the temperature 18 degrees, and a brisk wind picked up. Another 50 feet and 12 more degrees. We moved up a finger running down into the valley and encountered a snow squall halfway up. Once we were into the meadow, the sun broke out (after a rainstorm) and the temperature raised 15 degrees. This is mountain weather.

Altitude is another threat. It may take you six weeks to become 95-percent acclimatized to altitude. However, after only 10 days you will be about 80-percent acclimatized. So the 15-percent difference (which is substantial) will take you around four and one-half weeks to make up. At the border of very high and extreme altitude—18,000 feet—someone who is not acclimatized will find that his blood will only be saturated with oxygen at about 70 percent, versus the standard 95 percent at sea level. Less oxygen in your blood means that your ability to perform work and think will be drastically reduced. Additionally, you become susceptible to altitude illnesses.

Hypoxia, the state that results from a sustained reduced level of oxygen in the body, is what we are talking about. There are three types of altitude sickness: acute mountain sickness (AMS), high altitude pulmonary edema (HAPE), and high altitude cerebral edema (HACE).

AMS shows up at about 8,000 feet and will usually appear in less than 72 hours after your arrival at altitude, then dissipate within a few days (up to six). The classic symptoms include headache, fluid retention (peripheral edema), poor or labored sleep patterns, malaise, cyanosis due to reduced oxygen in the bloodstream, and nausea (including vomiting and a reduced appetite). You have two courses of action: stay put for two or three days and the symptoms may subside, or descend to the altitude at which you first started getting symptoms. If you stay, greatly increase your water intake and try the standard headache remedies. If you descend, you should do the very same thing. Also, should you elect to gut it out, reduce your work output as much as is feasible until your body adjusts.

AMS can progress into HAPE and is much more serious. In addition to AMS symptoms, expect a vicious cough with phlegm (remember that HAPE is a build-up of fluid in the lungs), fatigue, labored breathing after the slightest exertion along with cardiac and respiratory rate increase, and ataxia (obvious muscle coordination problems). A bystander may be able to hear the fluid in the victim's lungs (rales). Also, Cheyne-Stokes respiration (which could also be present in

AMS) may be pronounced. This is a weird respiratory malfunction that occurs during sleep. The victim's respiratory rate slowly increases until it reaches a crescendo, and then it stops completely for up to a minute, upon which time it resumes and the process starts again. Two to four days is the onset time for HAPE. It rarely shows up at altitudes below 8,000 feet.

Treatment is simple: descend immediately until symptoms disappear. Only those with minor cases of HAPE should ascend immediately after recovery. All others should seek medical attention if possible.

HACE will kill you if you fail to descend *right away*. This is a swelling of the brain that most often occurs at altitudes over 12,000 feet, but it can occur at anything over 10,000 feet. AMS symptoms—paralysis, convulsions, hallucinations, and extreme languor (weariness)—are all indicators of HACE. Descend now or risk death. This is not funny.

Before we shut the door on mountains as obstacles, remember that the one sure method of reducing altitude illnesses is to descend. Be alert; know what to look for. Act quickly.

Jungles, deserts, rain forests, and other ecosystems also manifest themselves as obstacles to evaders who are inexperienced in dealing with them. As with all obstacles, planning is the key to success.

ROADS AND RAILS

In this section we'll discuss those terrain features that man has arranged for the evader without intending for them to become impediments to his evasion. These include any path, trail, road, highway, house, farm, village, town, suburb, or city, plus anything else man has put in your way.

Paths, trails, and all thoroughfares, be they a country road up in the Bob Marshall Wilderness or an eight-lane interstate highway, are potential trouble spots. Humans are basically lazy creatures that will readily convince themselves that the convenient method of travel (roads, trails . . .) is sometimes acceptable, and even preferred, rather than stick it out and stay in the bush. Evaders who travel like this are unlikely to be evaders for much longer. And the evader who crosses a road or trail without regard for camouflage and concealment will soon join the former.

In hill country and mountains, roads are seldom straight, so you are probably going to have to cross at a curve. Before you sprint across, after listening for a few moments for approaching vehicles, crawl into a safe place that allows you to see in both directions. Observe the road for as long as possible to determine traffic patterns. Cross at night whenever possible, too. Be well camouflaged, taking special care to break up your outline. Your final position should be well-concealed as close to the side of the road as possible. (Did you bother to look for a culvert to use, instead of the road's surface?) Be sure to wipe out all your tracks leading up to the edge. When you cross, do so on all fours as quickly as possible. Do not run across upright! Nothing in the woods—with the possible exception of a Sasquatch—looks like a man running across a road except a man running across a road. If you scamper across on all fours, someone who sees you from a distance is likely to think you were a bear, coyote, deer, or some other critter instead of a man.

Straight stretches of road that offer shadows and low points on the roadsides (ditches, low shoulders) are what you want to find. Study your topographic map carefully for possible crossing spots.

You may have to cross a railroad bed. The same rules apply to railroads as to roads, but you can cross the tracks in another manner, which is to slither over the rails parallel to them instead of on all fours. Beware of hunters along the tracks; railroad beds are frequently used by game.

Homes, towns, and cities equate to a vastly increased chance of being seen and reported. You'd better have a real good reason for going anywhere near them. If you decide you absolutely must venture near them, *reconsider*. Am I coming across clearly? Stay away!

BEATING FIDO

Should your pursuers get wind of you and elect to employ dogs to track you or run you down, you've got a real problem. However, the evader *can* beat the dog if he uses his head and is able to use every available factor possible to defeat the dog or, better yet, the dog's handler.

The evader must use two things against the dog/handler team: terrain and weather. Both can be used to defeat either member of the team or both. Exceedingly rugged, treacherous terrain, hopefully adorned with thick, nasty vegetation, is not what either the dog or handler want to have to deal with (this is particularly true of the handler). Therefore, you want to go straight for this, and *fast*. Don't waste precious time sprinkling pepper or other distracters on the ground like you saw in the movies. Such things only present a minor and very temporary annoyance. They do not disable the dog.

Watery terrain is a worthy goal. Scent dogs key on fatty acids emitted by all humans or a recollection scent (as in a scent first experienced by a dog when he is allowed to sniff an article of clothing from a lost child). Scents are best detected and followed on windless, humid days. By traveling in water (streams, etc.) or over firm ground versus soft, the evader makes things tough on the dog's nose. If there is a stiff breeze and the humidity is low, the dog is going to have a hard time. Low humidity = greater evaporation = less scent near the ground. A stiff or gusty breeze = dissipation of scent. Water = no solid surface for the scent to accumulate on.

Then throw in obstacles like harsh terrain and plenty of thickets, and you have a dog that is having a bad time and a handler that is pissed off. This is precisely what you want.

But what if you find yourself being closely pursued by a loose dog bent on relieving you of some flesh and blood? Get your knife out.

If up-close-and-personal contact with the dog is imminent (read: you are about to be attacked), grasp your fixed- or lock-blade knife in your strong hand behind your back. Get low with one leg back, your weight distributed mostly to the rear. Have your weak arm parallel to the ground in front of your face. This you will present to the dog. Yes, you are going to give it to him, but only for a moment. Trust me here.

Most attack dogs are trained to go for the nearest arm or the arm with a weapon in it; hence your knife behind your back. When he bites into your weak arm, thrust your entire body forward and up, while bringing the knife swiftly from behind your back and into the dog's midsection, ideally just below where the ribs join at the sternum. Continue forward and get your body onto the dog's. Do not try and cut the dog's throat; dogs have excess fur and skin around their necks that can deflect or reduce the efficiency of your thrusts. Once the knife is in the dog's midsection, don't pull it out and try stabbing again. Instead, start carving without pulling the blade out. Keep your arm in the dogs mouth to stifle his cries (once you start eviscerating the dog, he will no longer be interested in biting you and will try to get free). A double-edged knife is preferable to a single in this case.

Hoist the dog's body over your shoulder and get out of there. Stash it well away from the kill site to reduce any sign of the killing. You may want to eat it.

Let's move on.

Chapter 9

Medicine Man

Medicinal herbalism has been around for as long as man himself. Our very distant fore-bears used various plants to treat everything from headaches to upper respiratory infections (URIs). Even today in our synthetic world, 25 percent of all drugs are derived wholly or in part from plants. A classic example of this is science's search for sources of taxol other than the Pacific yew (*Taxus brevifolia*), a.k.a. the western yew and mountain mahogany. Taxol is an anticancer drug which is extremely expensive, running about $1,000 per treatment phase. A patient may require nearly a dozen such treatment phases. Just a bit cost-prohibitive. Recently, medical science found the same taxol base in an obscure tree fungus. They are now trying to figure out how to get the fungus to produce larger quantities of the stuff so that the drug can be manufactured more cheaply.

But the evader is going to have to be much more than a medicinal herbalist. He must be adept at primitive first aid, too. Every time you become sick or injured, *you* are going to be the one to cure yourself. You can't return to society seeking medical help unless you are willing to run a serious risk of suspicion, recognition, or apprehension.

THE PHARMACOLOGICAL FLORIST

This section will be broken down by ailments and potential remedies. Some of these cures are historically proven; others are merely known to have been used by various peoples but have not been medically proven as truly effective. You must decide whether or not to try something listed herein. Also, you are the guy who is responsible for being able to identify each plant correctly and then use the right part of it in the right way, i.e., prepare the potion properly. The root of one plant might soothe your aching eyes, but the berries might kill you faster than Jim Jones' Kool-Aid. When you do your evasion area reconnaissance, take particular note of the plants. Bring samples back for identification or photograph them.

Allergies

Life-threatening? No. Maddeningly annoying? Oh, yeah. And if you were hiding in close proximity to a pursuer and were suddenly overcome by a sneezing fit brought on by pollen allergies, well, you get the picture.

Coltsfoot (*Tussilago farfara*) grows from coast to coast. However, don't confuse it with Canada wild ginger (*Asarum canadense*), which is sometimes known locally as coltsfoot. The two are different plants altogether. Boil one tablespoon of coltsfoot leaves in a cup of water and drink it. Do this several times daily. Coltsfoot helps reduce the inflammation of lung tissue caused by pollen allergies, calms the respiratory tract (mast cells), acts as an expectorant (makes you cough up mucus), and is a bronchial decongestant.

If you are up in northern New England (my neck of the woods), try elecampane (*Inula helenium*). Use the roots to make a tea; about one tablespoon of root per one cup of water. Elecampane is an expectorant and decongestant like coltsfoot, but it also has antibacterial properties and can prevent the terrible sneezing "fits" that strike allergy sufferers.

You're probably not going to believe this next one. Dandelion (*Taraxacum officinalis*), that damn yellow-flowered weed that is the bane of home owners everywhere, can be used to attack itself and other histamines. Again, one table-spoon of root per cup of water as a tea. Dandelion root taken in this manner steps up liver function. This in turn makes the liver remove the dandelion histamines in the pollen that is floating around your bloodstream.

Mullein (*Verbascum thapsus*), another weed, is also found nearly everywhere. Crush and dice the leaves until fine, then use the dried result as a tea: one tablespoon per cup of water several times a day. Mullein assists your lungs' alveoli and is a decongestant/expectorant.

If you are evading in the American Southwest, find some Mormon tea (*Ephedra viridis*). Fairly common in west Texas and other dry regions of the Southwest, it acts as a general decongestant. Use the same formula as the others. The young terminal growth is what you want.

Fevers

European barberry (*Berberis vulgaris*), found from the Midwest to the northeastern United States, has reddish-purple berries that can reduce fever. Take them raw or mash them into a drink. This perennial shrub is sometimes known as sow berry, dragon grape, and yellow root.

With about the same range as European barberry, wild indigo (*Baptisia tincoria*) was used by settlers to break fever. They boiled the root and drank the result. Also known as rattleweed, its roots are best used in the fall. You may find that the root is a bit laxative.

Common chokecherry (*Prunus virginiana*) has been used for a variety of ailments. For fevers, scrape some root bark into boiling water, let it steep, and drink.

Blue vervain (*Verbena hastate*) likes just about all areas except the desert. Boil the roots and drink the tea to increase perspiration/reduce low-grade fevers. Take only a little at first, as it may act as a purgative.

Wounds

The faster a wound heals, the less chance it has of becoming infected. A number of plants in North America speed healing.

Yarrow (*Achilles millefolium*) grows nearly everywhere in the United States and has several uses, one of which is healing wounds. Make a poultice out of the lacy leaves and apply to lacerations, punctures, and abrasions.

Sweetgum (*Liquidambar styraciflua*) is a common tree in the East and South. The star-shaped leaves are unmistakable, as are the round, spiked seed capsules. Boil the leaves and apply them to the wound.

The eastern white pine (*Pinus strobus*) is also very common in eastern America, though it is found more to the north. It, too, is hard to mistake. Native Americans once used the softened bark to foster healing.

Common juniper (*Juniperus communis*) is another conifer used by Native Americans who applied a poultice of the stems and needles to wounds.

In drier locales such as eastern Washington and Utah, big sagebrush (*Artemisia tridentata*) was used by Native Americans to treat lacerations and other wounds. The leaves were boiled and the liquid poured over the wound.

Jimson weed (*Datura meteloides*), and jimsonweed (*Datura stramonium*) were both used by Native Americans for a variety of reasons. Both have narcotic/hallucinogenic properties, so care must be taken; i.e. don't consume any part of them when considering them for medicinal uses. Instead, make a poultice of the leaves and apply it to the wound.

Constipation

This is no laughing matter when you're trying to survive and evade.

Plantain (*Plantago*) is that broad-leafed weed with the erect seed spikes growing in your lawn. The seeds are an outstanding laxative. Roast them or eat them raw. The leaves are good to nibble on, too.

White turtlehead (*Chalone glabra*) is found in much of the East's wetter regions. The leaves can be dried, ground, and powdered, then taken as a laxative.

Much of the eastern half of the country is home to black walnut (*Juglans nigra*), whose inner bark can be eaten as a laxative. Crush the walnuts and drink the juice for the same effect, but not too much. Like the cigarette cure for tapeworms (eat the tobacco from *one* cigarette and you will rid yourself of worms, though it is a violent solution), black walnut juice will kill intestinal parasites.

Black oak (*Quercus velutina*) bark can be soaked and eaten to loosen your bowels.

EMERGENCY SITUATIONS

When evading with others for any length of time, you are going to incur injuries no matter how many precautions you take to thwart them. This means that you are going to be the doctor. Before you head out into the backwoods, I suggest you take more than a basic first aid course. Evaders need more than the basics when it comes to emergency medicine.

Patient Assessment

Before you commence treatment, you have to know what is wrong. And before you determine what is wrong, you have to get the patient to a position of safety if he is in a precarious situation. The base of a cliff is not the place to treat a patient. Falling rocks and other debris will ruin your good work.

If the victim appears unconscious, yell at him from a few feet away (get too close while doing this, and you may find yourself with a fist or knife in the face). If you receive no response, shake him gently (unless you suspect a spinal injury).

Now you have to do your ABCs: open the airway, check for breathing (watch the chest to see if it is rising and falling, put your ear to the mouth and nose to listen for air moving), and feel for the carotid pulse on the side of the neck. Also check the brachial, i.e., wrist pulse. A = airway/B = breathing/C = circulation. Cardiopulmonary resuscitation (CPR) should be applied if a heartbeat is absent. You do know CPR, right?

Bleeding must be stopped. Don't sweat the capillary bleeding (minor, slowly oozing). However, venous (dark red, flowing blood) and arterial (bright red, spurting blood) bleeding must be stopped immediately. Direct pressure on the wound, elevation of the wound, or a pressure point may be used. Maybe all three. Unless you want the victim to lose a limb, don't use a tourniquet. A complete shut-off of blood to a limb for only a few hours will mean amputation if the victim survives. Tourniquets are out (unless all other methods fail).

Finally, there is shock, the mind's refusal to accept what has happened to the body. Always treat for shock, regardless of the severity of the injury. Keep the victim calm, warm, and treated. Extremes of temperature in either direction must be avoided. Elevate the legs so that the blood returns easily to the heart and brain; 10 inches is about right. Keep an eye on the heart! Shock is caused by the heart's inability to get blood (carrying oxygen) to the tissues.

Once you have the victim stabilized, that is, out of immediate danger from the injuries and what caused them, you should check the entire body closely for other injuries. Know how to find the problem (if it isn't obvious), treat it, and follow up. Have a plan in mind. Be proactive.

Chapter 10

Stranger in a Strange Land

You may decide, after some very long and careful thought, that evasion for you will best be conducted outside the United States and Canada. There are plenty of wild places to evade on this planet. But no matter which region or country you select—the Australian Outback, Mindoro, India, Ecuador, or Namibia—you will still run the same risks of detection, only they will now be greatly increased. You are a stranger in a strange land, an outsider. Outsiders appear to be just that, especially when they are trying hard not to appear as outsiders or to hide. The answer is to avoid suspicion by not appearing to hide.

American prisoners of war who were held in Hoa Lo prison in Hanoi during the Vietnam War (and perhaps thereabouts after the war was supposedly ended) had a similar debacle. In the words of one former POW, a Navy commander (then lieutenant) who had his F4 Phantom jet blown out from underneath him by a surface-to-air missile (SAM) in 1968, the prisoners could have been ". . . running around the streets of Hanoi . . ." just about any night they saw fit. Escape was that easy. The problem, though, was what they were to do once they were outside. No friendly forces were nearby. They were in bad physical condition due to poor nutrition, medical neglect, and torture. And they all looked just a little bit different than the rest of the populace. They would have stuck out like the proverbial sore thumbs.

The evader's answer is to be casual, and not appear to be suspicious or surreptitious. However, you must remain on guard, too.

But first you have to get out of this country. Don't leave via the usual method, i.e., the airport or driving. A tramp steamer might be of use. Roughly $250 in the hand of the captain, particularly a non-American (preferably third world) sailing under a foreign flag, will probably keep his mouth shut. Another method is to slip into Mexico. Be careful here. The crossing area (exactly where you go under the fence) is crucial. Border patrol and DEA agents use thermal imaging devices and night observation devices (NODS) to monitor the fence. Have cash on hand to bribe your way to a port of exit (preferably by sea).

Once you are safely in your evasion region and you are sure you weren't detected leaving the United States and left no indicators of your destination, you can go about your business. Your cover story while in-country will depend on numerous factors. Just keep it simple and believable. You're a hiker on sabbatical from a university. You're a wildlife photographer. You're on vacation from your job at an automobile plant. Whatever works.

THE LOCALS

You will run into three different types of people: those who are indifferent, those who are friendly and helpful, and those who are suspicious or outright hostile.

The first type are definitely the most dangerous, because you don't know what they are going to do. Yes, this is also true of the other two types, but indifferent people make the hair on the back of my neck stand up, you know? They are tough to read and, therefore, a threat. Get away from them as fast as possible. Leave in one direction (making sure he or she sees you going that way), and then, as soon as the situation permits, alter your course radically, covering your tracks as you go. The military term is "break contact."

Obviously suspicious or openly hostile people also present a clear threat. Do not respond to them in a like manner. Break contact politely and as quickly as possible. Again, depart the area so that they see you going one way, then change your heading.

Friendly people should also be considered a potential threat, as appearances can be deceiving. Never do or say anything that might come off as suspicious. Be polite and conversant, but don't linger too long. Don't ask them questions about themselves, as this may put them on the defensive. When you leave, ask for directions to a certain area, head that way, then change your heading as soon as you can.

Your evasion area reconnaissance should have included a study of social, economic, religious, political, and cultural aspects of people indigenous to the region. By knowing how not to offend, you make yourself more welcome. Conceal all weapons. Show deference to all, especially women and children. Appear genuinely interested in what they have to say, but try to avoid comments on politics and religion.

Courtesy will often save the day. If food is offered, eat it. Forget your own cultural taboos. If they offer you broiled slugs, eat them. Lose the nasty facial expressions. Eat what is offered, but don't make a pig of yourself. In Islamic regions, never take or serve food with the left hand. Shake hands whenever you meet someone and again when you leave. Don't rush anything. Take your time.

In markets, don't pay the first price asked. Dicker, then pay a lesser—but still reasonable—price. Barter is acceptable in many less-developed nations. Any U.S. currency is good, plus unusual items and even items that you would think are commonplace. Your Timex watch, pocket knife, sunglasses, T-shirt, cigarettes, razor blades, and who knows what else may strike someone's fancy.

Conduct your business and leave. Don't hang around.

Don't be overly loud or act obnoxious in any way. In other words, do nothing that would make the memory of you stick out in someone's mind. I have read that gold is a great barter item. For nonevaders, this might be true. But for evaders, gold is out unless it is a common barter item. Even then, never flash large quantities of gold. Not only will you be memorable, but you run the very serious risk of being waylaid by dirtbags.

If time permits, learn some of the language before entering the region. Once there, always expand your ability to speak, read, and understand it. A little knowledge of the language shows respect for a people's culture and heritage. They will immediately know you are not one of them, and they will probably ask where you are from. Canada is a good answer for Americans. You'd better have some specifics ready, too. Do you have any Canadian currency with you?

Before you shove off, check the library for the latest information on your selected region one last time. Check for political unrest and terrorism. Carefully contact the State Department for info, too.

The Bug-Out Bag

I f you live in a precarious situation which requires you to be ready to institute your evasion plan of action on a moment's notice, you must have a "bug-out" bag ready. This might be in the form of a large pack (minimum of 4,500-cubic-inch capacity) or some other easy-to-transport system. What you have in that bag has to be sufficient for you to survive and evade for two weeks, at least. An outstanding idea to supplement this bag is to have caches already strategically located in your evasion area.

Both your bug-out bag and your supplemental system (caches) must be thought of in broad, comprehensive terms. Also, they must be set up in a "worst case" scenario. Don't plan for good luck. Evaders must always plan for the worst. That way, when luck does come your way, it is pure gravy. Your bug-out bag should be complied with two things in mind: the environment you are heading into (tundra, jungle, mountains, and so on) and your personal needs (eyeglasses, medication, and such).

THE KOPPEN-GEIGER SYSTEM

The Koppen-Geiger System is a method of climatic classification that breaks down regions by average precipitation and temperatures in a month, season, or year. This gives us five primary climates: ice, snow, warm temperate, dry, and tropical.

Ice Climates

These are regions where the warmest summer months mean temperature never goes above 49°F. We are talking about the polar and subpolar regions for the most part. Seasonal variations are just about nonexistent.

Snow Climates

In a snow climate, the average temp for the coldest month falls below 26.6°F. Most of Canada and Alaska, plus a good portion of the upper Midwest and Northeast, fall into this category. Seasons are only moderately defined, at best.

Warm, Temperate Climates

These are middle-of-the-road regions, where the coldest month of the year sees temperatures averaging under 64.4°F, but above 26.6°F. The difference in seasons is clear.

Dry Climates

Dry climates have less to do with strict temperature guidelines. Instead, evaporation is the key. These areas all show evaporation potential getting the best of all types of precipitation for most of the year. This means that intermittent (seasonal) streams and lakes are the norm, with no perennial bodies of water at all. Seasons are fairly well-defined.

Tropical Climates

Perhaps you have heard it said that man is a tropical animal. He is indeed. He can only survive unclothed year-round in the tropics—the Tropic of Capricorn and the Tropic of Cancer. He needs clothing everywhere else. In the tropics, the mean monthly temperature all year long is above 64.4°F, and evaporation can't keep up with precipitation. Spring and fall are recognizable, but a true winter isn't.

Elevation

In all these regions you will find elevation extremes. Expect marked differences in what you find as you ascend. Snowcapped mountains in the desert are common, as are other seeming contradictions.

• • • • •

Now that you know what category your evasion area falls into, you can set up your bag accordingly. Everything you stuff in there should be meant to assist in either a medical, navigation, fire-building, shelter-construction, signaling, or food-and-water-procurement mode. These six skill areas are what the evader must be good at in order to defeat threats to his survival. Shortcomings in any one of them can prove deadly.

PERSONAL NEEDS

Your bug-out bag should be designed not only for evasion, but for survival as well. This means that personal medications, glasses, and other items unique to your needs must be in there. Personal medications may have expiration dates, and other items may also have a limited shelf life. Such materials need to be replaced in a timely manner so that your bug-out bag is truly "ready to go" at all times.

In addition to these special items, prepare the bag to help you deal with threats to your survival and safe evasion. You have to know who and what your enemies are. If you don't, your evasion will likely never get off the ground.

These threats are illnesses and injuries, temperature extremes, hunger, thirst, fatigue, loneliness/boredom, and fear. Every evader will experience at least one of these threats, probably more. They may come singly or several at once. But they will come. The one you are least prepared for is usually the one that shows up first at the worst possible time.

I will not try to list everything you are going to require. However, I'll give you some good ideas to work with, which will serve as a starting point and as food for thought. Remember that your bug-out bag *absolutely must be customized for you* and only you. There is no such thing as a generic bug-out bag. Anything you read that contradicts this is not worth reading.

Medical Gear

Stock your medical kit well right from the get-go. Think about the climate you are heading into, and think about extremes in that climate. Now put in there what you think you'll need. A wide variety is what you're looking for, along with plenty of each item if they are expendable. Every cache you lay in should have medical resupplies.

Navigation

Two high-quality compasses (pack an extra one in case your primary compass breaks or is lost), topographic maps (and adjoining sheets), and sketches you have made for caches and other reasons will make up this section. Waterproof all maps and sketches by applying acetate to them. Wet maps and sketches will come apart.

Fire Building

The fire section of your bag must be designed to work under especially bad conditions. Have a variety of high-quality tinder, kindling, and even some smaller fuel bundles in there. Butane lighters, strike-anywhere kitchen matches in a solid waterproof container, a metal match, magnesium block with built-in striker, 35mm film canisters crammed with petroleum jelly-coated cotton balls, synthetic tinder/kindling sticks, and steel wool are all good choices. Don't skimp on this section.

Shelter Construction

A hefty wad of nylon "550" parachute cord, a tarpaulin, plastic sheeting, and an assortment of nails and spikes will all come in very handy. Tents are out. Evaders who want to stay such don't use tents.

Signaling

You'll need audio and visual signals: two good miniature flashlights with extra bulbs and batteries, a compact short-wave radio and extra batteries (waterproof the radio), a lightweight, compact flare gun or pencil flare, a rugged plastic whistle, and so on.

Food and Water Procurement

There are some excellent water filters/purifiers on the market that are destined for your bag. The PUR Explorer ($130), MSR Waterworks ($140), First Need Deluxe ($48), and Katadyn Pocket Water Filter ($225) are all good. Chemical purifiers such as iodine tablets (Polar Pure, $8.50) and Potable Aqua (tetraglycine hydroperiodide) should also be in there. Potable Aqua runs about $3 for a bottle of 50 tablets. Have some clear plastic bags for rigging transpiration bags, vegetation stills, and solar stills. Include a long piece of surgical tubing for sucking the water out.

Snare wire, a fishing kit (complete with lures, line, hooks, sinkers, commercially prepared baits, et al), weapons and ammunition, and skinning, deboning, and butchering knives are all meant for your food and water section. So is a book on edible plants, plus a set of small cooking utensils and vessels.

What else? Whatever you see fit.

Vanishing Act

The two villagers were supposed to be on the trail that runs from the treeline across from the prison camp down into the valley when the prison work crew and their guards would be coming down the trail on their daily wood-cutting excursion. They would take down the unsuspecting guards and make tracks for the valley as fast as possible with the four prisoners, then link up with the special operations team hidden and waiting in the forest.

The team was in place when the first villager came into view as he stepped from the trees along a swollen stream. The man gave the prearranged signal in the direction of the thicket on the other side of the stream, and, seeing nothing in return (no return signal *was* the countersignal), continued on across, the prisoners right behind him and the second villager bringing up the rear.

Disappearing into the thicket, I could hear them making their way toward me. The first villager passed within 4 feet of me and gave me a sly grin as our eyes met in the shadows. He slid by and then came the first prisoner. I leaned forward and gave a barely discernible whistle as his head emerged from around a spruce tree. He turned his head and found himself looking right into my eyes, only inches from his own.

My right forefinger was pressed vertically against my green and brown lips, giving the silence signal that everyone is familiar with. The look on his face was one of shock and amazement. He obviously wasn't expecting to see a lizardlike creature awaiting him in the woods, but I was there nonetheless. The remainder of the team was all around me, but he wasn't allowed to see them until the four prisoners were secure and the two villagers "cleared." Ten minutes later the newly freed men were on a helicopter and heading for home.

Camouflage is a long-practiced art that has been used by man and his forerunners for many millennia. It comes in an astounding array of forms and variations, from the undercover cop dressed as a homeless man sleeping in a filthy alley in Brooklyn to the backcountry game warden lying in wait beside a remote alpine meadow, covered head to foot with foliage as camouflage, waiting for the elk poacher he knows will be there soon. The evader who is anything less than a master at camouflage will soon be a former evader.

EIGHT STEPS TO TOTAL CONCEALMENT

Camouflage is much more than applying some face paint and a few pieces of brush to your body. It is a concept—a science and an art all in one. The evader must practice his art in 10 different areas if he expects to be truly evasive concealment-wise.

Movement
When in doubt, freeze.

That is some of the soundest advice I can give you on this matter. Man is a predator, and you must always remember that when evading. His senses all complement one another, but sight is one of his best. The human eye is naturally attracted to movement, and even the smallest flicker will get his attention fast. If you hunt, you know precisely what I am talking about. Intuition tells you that a deer is standing in a thicket, but you can't quite make it out. You watch the thicket intently and then see the slightest twitch of an ear. Suddenly the entire deer materializes before you and you wonder how you didn't see it sooner.

This is why night movement is often wiser than day movement. Humans have comparatively poor eyesight come sundown, and evaders should use this to their advantage as much as possible. But the show fits both feet. Night movement can be treacherous, to say the least. Unseen objects such as gravel, branches, and ice all can be accidentally trodden upon by the evader, and they all make noise when crushed. Noise travels farther during hours of darkness, generally speaking. A snapped twig that would go unnoticed 100 meters away during the day might be heard clearly at 200 meters at night.

Noise is not the only danger, of course. Hazards like ravines, holes, cliffs, and potentially dangerous wildlife are all waiting for the careless evader. Caution and common sense will help the evader immensely. The use of a probing stick slightly taller than one's self is highly advisable. Shorten your steps substantially during night movement, and put the balls of your feet down first, versus the heels. Continue to use whatever nature provides to break up your outline, just as you would during day movement. Stay off the skyline at all times. If you must cross a ridge crest, crawl over it. Never silhouette yourself, even for a moment. A crescent moon on a clear night sheds more light than many realize.

You should move with a plan in mind, a well-thought-out plan than uses the terrain and vegetation to your advantage. Don't just shoot a bearing with your compass and strike out. Animals don't move through the wilderness in a straight line, and you shouldn't either. They creep, slink, crawl, and slither from one locale to the next. Take the hint.

If you have a map, hopefully a topographic map, use it. Study it. Become an expert at recognizing the subtle nuances of the map and its representative terrain. Could you move along the military crest (the away side of a ridge just below the topographic crest) of that esker, thus avoiding exposing yourself to the trail intersection below? Will that shallow saddle (the low ground between two hills) allow you to pass out of the valley and into the range beyond without risking detection from the village off to the east?

As you travel, avoid using vegetation to assist your ascent or descent. A sapling or branch moving suddenly on an otherwise still day will get someone's attention instantly. And should that object break, the resounding SNAP! could be heard for quite a ways. Squirrel hunters look for moving branches that let them know their prey is up there somewhere. Someone looking for you will also be looking for moving branches, bent-back boughs, and bent-over young trees.

Your movement may go unseen by other humans, but those same humans may see the effects of your movement manifested in other ways. If you spook an elk and it goes crashing off through the timber, anyone nearby may see it and wonder what set the big deer to flight. (Yes, elk *are* deer.) So you see, you are dealing with not only man—who may or may not be adept in the wilds—but also the indigenous creatures that have dwelt thereabouts all their lives. The mistakes you can make are myriad.

If you recall the movie *Caddyshack*, you saw Chevy Chase playing a golf wizard. At one point he tells his protégé: "Be the ball, Danny." What he was trying to get Danny to do was get in mental and physical "sync" with the ball, to make happen what he wanted to happen. In evasion, the evader must "be the bush," "be the stream," "be the rock." When you make a mistake in movement, freeze! Then slowly dissolve your outline by sinking to the ground and becoming as small as possible. Turn your face *away* from the danger area. Never look directly in the direction of the threat. Eye contact must be avoided.

Stay frozen until you are absolutely sure all is safe. Then slowly, ever so slowly, continue on.

Position

Precisely how the evader positions himself is a factor that

is easy to overlook. Predatory animals, such as barracuda, are experts at positioning. They blend in with their background, thus making themselves much more difficult to detect. Many camouflage clothing manufacturers have capitalized on this theory and are making patterns that "melt" into the vegetation and terrain in general—patterns that look like tree bark or a bush complete with leaves, branches, and twigs. Even berries are included in the most intricate patterns. They are making good use of position, but the wearer only gets the maximum benefit from such clothing if he is still and right up against the vegetation, rocks, water's edge, or what have you.

Color and Contrast

Color is relative, meaning how well it actually assists in concealing you depends on who or what is looking for you. Red would not be the color of choice for daytime evasion, but it is very useful come nightfall. The color red is at the long end of the light wavelength. On a dark, moonless night, it appears black to the human eye. Green can appear white or light yellow. Blue also appears white. Strange but true.

Contrast is something you must take into account, too. Subtle blending is what you are looking for, especially at close range. The further you are from a possible pursuer, the less you need to be concerned with contrast.

Minimal contrast, when applied with restricted movement and proper color, goes a long way toward making you disappear, particularly at night. While on a reconnaissance mission in an Asian jungle one night many years ago, my team point man and I were crawling through an open field amid the dense jungle so we could get a better look at some individuals who were gathered in the clearing around a small fire.

We were about 30 meters from the group when my partner, mere inches behind me, tapped me on the foot twice. This meant that someone was coming up behind us. Silently we rolled aside in different directions and froze.

Seconds passed. Then minutes. Finally, four men filed

past and joined the group in the clearing. I had no idea how my partner detected them so far off, but found out later that he had heard them coming up the streambed. The heavily-armed men had walked right between us and never knew we were there. Subtle coloration and hues, minimal contrast, and no movement made us invisible to the men. If any of them saw us lying on either side of them, we probably appeared as logs.

Shine

This is one factor that leaves little room for error. Shine can be seen for miles under the right conditions. During hours of darkness, shine that may not have been noticed in day can become like a beacon. Water, some antlers, and certain types of rock have the ability to shine under the right conditions. However, shine in nature is an attention-getter. Eyes are drawn to it.

One error in shine can end it all. I have seen near-perfectly camouflaged men and equipment in the desert be detected instantly when they were otherwise unseen, all because of a vehicle mirror that was not turned down and away from the rising sun. One mistake was all it took.

Eyeglasses are a big offender. So are knife blades, watches, aluminum cans, rings, belt buckles, and other seemingly harmless items. Note that all have smooth surfaces that readily reflect even the weakest light. Texture, i.e. "roughing up" the surface of these objects, will help. Caution and prevention are vital, and you can easily prevent shine from giving you away by not wearing watches and rings (keep them in your pocket), and by paying attention to what is exposed to light. Staying in the shadows greatly reduces the chances of shine ruining your day, forever.

Shadow

Professional snipers know that despite Hollywood's ideas, you don't hang out windows and engage targets. You stay a few steps back into the room to take full advantage of the natural concave shadow that is formed by a room. Shadows are a natural asset to the evader.

But a shadow can also be a detractor—your shadow, that is. Your outline should be broken up by any means available that appear natural. If your outline is taken care of, the shadow will be as well. Late afternoon is the time when your shadow can work against you. On the other hand, if you are crafty and have disguised your shadow, this time of day can be beneficial.

Gamekeepers in the British Isles used to employ a method of camouflage called the ghillie. It is a shapeless garment made of tidbits of dull cloth that blends in with the environment. Draped over the body, it obscures any recognizable shadow, too. Remember, you want to appear as little like a human as possible. The human eye is trained to quickly recognize many shapes, especially that of another human.

Tone

Tone has to do with a single color and the phases of that color. The key is one of the aforementioned camouflage recognition factors, contrast. It has three parts: the color itself, the amount of light available, and the shade of the color.

You can create the right tone if you can govern these three factors. If one escapes you, tone is lost. The late Ansel Adams, the master of black and white nature photography, was an expert at tone management. His photos of Yosemite and other places of natural wonder demonstrated a remarkable understanding of tone as seen through the lens. This same mastery can be applied to camouflage.

You can tone yourself down by countering drastic differences in color and using texture to mask contrasts. Mud applied to the face, hands, and neck uses texture to counter the tone of your skin. Burlap and wool garments have their own texture that does the same thing for your clothing.

Shape

The evader's silhouette is the clearest example I can give on this topic. We are talking about outline as opposed to color. But you don't have to be on the geographical crest of a hill or ridge to have your shape compromise you. Broad daylight will do it, too.

Animals recognize man by scent and sight, though they may *detect* him by hearing as well. Prey and predator alike use a man's shape as the key visual factor in recognition. Your shape is your identification card; you have to alter it.

The head and shoulders, arms and upper torso, and legs and hips all form separate shapes that can cause your recognition independently of one another. These shapes must be broken up by strategically placed vegetation or clothing. Also, by using smart movement techniques, you can avoid shape recognition, i.e., walking upright through the forest understory for extended distances is asking for trouble. Move from tree to bush to rock to ravine. Crawl if you must, but lose your shape.

Epilogue

I have found that once a man comes to the end of a journey, he tends to look back and judge what has transpired and what he has accomplished. I am confident that you, too, will find yourself looking back with an array of memories, good and not so good, when you have completed your evasion successfully. You will see all the mistakes you made early on, and wonder how you could have been so stupid—and careless. And you will marvel at how you were able to continue on without being caught by the enemy.

This book started out by stressing the importance of planning. I am compelled to do so again now, at the end. My friend, you had better plan your evasion with the utmost care and thought. Small mistakes and oversights will get you caught or killed. I have come so close to being caught by people I was trying to remain undetected by that my heart still races from time to time when I get to thinking about how my lack of planning, carelessness, laziness, stupidity, and sometimes just plain bad luck nearly turned disastrous. I recall the time my recon team and I were all nearly nabbed because I failed to set out security as we neared a road. I never made that mistake a second time, and that is another key to your success: never make the same mistake twice.

You must strive not to be deficient in any skill area. The skill you are a little short on is the one you will need the most at the worst possible time.

FINAL THOUGHTS

Think before you act, but trust your instincts. Choose your evasion group members very carefully; your life depends on your judgment. All shortcuts lead down the path of doom. When in doubt, shoot to kill, but have a means of escape, and never believe for a second that dead men tell no tales; they tell whole volumes to he who would listen.

Subtlety is the lifeblood of the evader, but boldness and audacity are his trump cards when things get dicey.

Learn the ways of nature. She will provide for he who takes what she offers—and strike down the man who hesitates. Robert W. Service, in his eerie poem *The Law of the Yukon*, said it all:

> *Wild and wide are my borders,*
> *stern as death is my sway;*
> *From my ruthless throne I have ruled alone*
> *for a million years and a day . . .*
> *I am the land that listens,*
> *I am the land that broods;*
> *Steeped in eternal beauty,*
> *crystalline waters and woods.*